Eastern HEMISPHERE

WORKBOOK

This ancillary can be used with the 1995 copyright.

Silver Burdett Ginn
Parsippany, NJ • Needham, MA
Atlanta, GA   Deerfield, IL   Irving, TX   Santa Clara, CA

Contents

For textbook chapter		Use Workbook pages
	Using Your Textbook	3–10
	Map Skills Handbook	11–18
Chapter 1	Ancient Civilizations in the Middle East and Egypt	19–24
Chapter 2	Ancient Greece	25–30
Chapter 3	Ancient Rome	31–37
Chapter 4	Ancient India and China	38–43
Chapter 5	Geography of Western Europe	44–48
Chapter 6	History of Western Europe	49–54
Chapter 7	Three Revolutions	55–60
Chapter 8	Nationalism and Two World Wars	61–64
Chapter 9	Western Europe Today	65–68
Chapter 10	Geography of the Former Soviet Union and Eastern Europe	69–71
Chapter 11	History of Russia and Eastern Europe	72–75
Chapter 12	The Former Soviet Union and Eastern Europe Today	76–79
Chapter 13	Geography of the Middle East and North Africa	80–83
Chapter 14	History of the Middle East and North Africa	84–87
Chapter 15	The Middle East and North Africa Today	88–92
Chapter 16	Geography of Africa South of the Sahara	93–97
Chapter 17	History of Africa South of the Sahara	98–101
Chapter 18	Africa South of the Sahara Today	102–106
Chapter 19	Geography of South and East Asia	107–110
Chapter 20	History of South and East Asia	111–114
Chapter 21	South and East Asia Today	115–120
Chapter 22	Geography of Australia, New Zealand, and the Pacific Islands	121–124
Chapter 23	Past and Present in Australia, New Zealand, and the Pacific Islands	125–128

2 3 4 5 6 7 8 9 - PO - 05 04 03 02 01 00 99 98 97

© 1997 Silver Burdett Ginn Inc. All rights reserved.
Printed in the United States of America.
The publisher hereby grants permission to reproduce these
pages, in part or in whole, for classroom use only.
ISBN 0-382-32714-4

NAME _____

WHERE DOES THAT CHAPTER BEGIN?

USING THE TABLE OF CONTENTS

If you wanted to turn to Chapter 7 in your textbook, how would you find it? You could turn the pages until you come to Chapter 7, but an easier way would be to look in the front of the book at the Table of Contents.

The Table of Contents shows you how the textbook is divided into units and chapters. It lists the titles of the units and chapters and gives the page numbers of each chapter. The subjects discussed in each chapter are listed below the chapter title. The Table of Contents also shows where maps, graphs, diagrams, literature excerpts, and other special features are located in the textbook.

✱ Use the Table of Contents in your textbook to answer the questions below.

1. In which unit would you read about the ancient civilizations of Greece and Rome? _____

2. On what page would you begin to read about the geography of Western Europe? _____

3. In which chapters would you find information about the Middle East and North Africa? _____

4. What subjects are discussed in Chapter 4? _____

5. On which page would you find a literature excerpt from *Ivanhoe*? _____

6. In which chapter would you read about Japan today? _____

7. In which chapter would you find information about the Industrial Revolution? _____

8. What subjects are discussed in Chapter 9? _____

Thinking Further: Write one or two sentences describing how a table of contents is like an outline you might prepare before writing a term paper.

_____
_____
_____
_____
_____

Table of Contents

NAME _____

WHERE IS THAT TOPIC DISCUSSED?

USING THE INDEX

The Index in the back of your textbook is a helpful tool. It gives an alphabetical listing of topics in the book and the pages on which they may be found. The topics are important people, places, and things. A person's name is listed last name first. The entry for a book title shows the last name of the author in parentheses. The entry for a ruler lists the country and title in parentheses. At the top of each page are two guide words. They list the first and last entries on that page so that you can find the entry you need quickly.

Some topics are divided into an entry word and one or more subentries. The entry word, which appears in dark print, is the main topic. The subentries, found below the entry word, highlight specific divisions of the main topic. Subentries are listed alphabetically by first important word. To find a topic, look in the Index under the most general heading first. For example, to find the pages on which the ancient civilization of Egypt is discussed, look at the entry word *Egypt* and at the subentry *ancient civilization of*. If no such entry exists, check the subentries under the word *civilization*.

✱ Use the Index in your textbook to answer the questions below.

1. On what pages would you find information on the plebeians? _____

2. On what pages would you find information about Joseph Stalin? _____

3. Under what main entry would you first look to find out where the Israeli Knesset is discussed? _____

4. Who is discussed first in your textbook, the Egyptian pharaoh Menes or the Roman emperor Augustus? _____

5. What is the subentry under the main entry *New Zealand*? _____

6. On what pages would you find information on the Magna Carta? _____

7. On what pages would you find information about World War I? _____

Thinking Further: The word *index* comes from a Latin verb that means "to indicate" or "to point to." How does this describe the function of an index?

_____
_____
_____
_____

Index, pages 648–659

NAME _____

WHAT DOES THAT WORD MEAN?

USING THE GLOSSARY

The Glossary in the back of your textbook lists each vocabulary term and the meaning that is used in the textbook. As you can see in the sample entries below, the Glossary also gives the page on which each word is first used and a pronunciation for the word.

The entries in the Glossary are in alphabetical order. Two guide words appear at the top of each page. They list the first and last entries on that page so that you can quickly find the vocabulary term you need.

> *cacao* (kuh KAY oh). The tree and the seeds from which cocoa and chocolate are made. p. 450.
> *caliph* (KAY lihf). The Arabic title given to Muslim religious leaders. p. 386.
> *calligraphy* (kuh LIHG ruh fee). The art of handwriting. p. 397.

✻ Use the Glossary in your textbook to answer the questions below.

1. What is the Glossary definition for the word *atoll*? _____
_____

2. Write the pronunciation for the word *Confucianism*. _____

3. What is the pronunciation for the word *protectorate*? _____

4. On what page of the textbook would you find the first mention of the word *jute*? _____

5. What are the guide words for the page that includes the word *longitude*? _____
_____

6. What is one basic similarity between Parliament and the Diet? _____
_____

7. Describe similarities and differences between a democracy and a monarchy. _____
_____
_____

Thinking Further: A gloss is a brief explanation of a word. How does this describe the function of a glossary? Write your answer on a separate sheet.

Glossary, pages 640–647

NAME _____

WHAT CAN I LEARN ABOUT THAT PLACE?

USING THE GAZETTEER

Have you ever heard the name of a place and wanted to know more about it? Would you like to know where the Congo River begins and ends? Would you like to find out where the ancient city of Carthage was located?

Answers to questions like these may be found in the Gazetteer in your textbook. A gazetteer is a dictionary of geographical terms. It is arranged like a glossary, in alphabetical order, with guide words at the top of each page. As you can see from the sample entries below, each entry first gives a pronunciation for the term. Then it describes the place and lists the page where you can find it on a map. The Gazetteer also lists latitude and longitude for cities and some other places.

> *Harappa* (huh RAP uh). Site of ancient city in the Indus Valley. (31°N/73°E) p. 129.
> *Harare* (hah RAH ree). Capital of Zimbabwe, in southern Africa. (18°S/31°E) p. 478.
> *Harbin* (HAHR bihn). City in northeastern China, on the Songhua River. (46°N/127°E) p. 617.

✻ Use the Gazetteer in your textbook to answer the questions below.

1. In what country is the city of Tripoli located? _____
2. Into what sea does the Yenisei River empty? _____
3. On what river is the Iraqi capital of Baghdad located? _____
4. On what page would you find the Bay of Bengal on a map? _____
5. What are the latitude and longitude of the city of Athens? _____
6. What is the highest peak of the Himalayas, and what is its elevation? _____
_____
7. What is the Great Dividing Range? _____
8. What is the former name of Beijing, the capital of China? _____
9. What is the pronunciation of the term *Iberian Peninsula*? _____

Thinking Further: Why is it useful that the Gazetteer gives you the page number of a map on which each place can be found?
_____
_____
_____

NAME _____

WHERE IS THAT PLACE LOCATED?

USING THE ATLAS

An atlas is a collection of maps. The Atlas in the back of your textbook has maps of the world and of continents. Both physical and political maps of these areas are shown. For Australia and New Zealand, physical and political features are shown on one map. Physical maps show important natural features, such as mountains and rivers. Political maps show the locations of boundaries and capitals and other cities. Both physical and political maps show latitude and longitude.

Some of the world maps in the Atlas are special-purpose maps. These maps show one thing about the areas on the map. A map showing the climate, precipitation, or products of a region is an example of a special-purpose map.

The physical maps and political maps in your Atlas each provide a scale of miles and kilometers for measuring distances. The maps have keys that show what the symbols on the maps represent.

✻ Use the Atlas in your textbook to answer the questions below.

1. On which map of North America would you look to find the names of the countries on that continent? _____

2. What is the national capital of the South American country of Peru? _____

3. On which map of North America would you find the names of the five Great Lakes, which are located on the border between Canada and the United States? _____
_____

4. What is the largest country in the land area of Eurasia, and which map of Eurasia shows this country's boundaries? _____
_____

5. What South American mountain range runs along the Pacific coast the entire length of the continent? _____

6. Look at the political map of Eurasia. On which body of water is the city of Bombay, India, located? _____

7. On the special-purpose map of the forests of the world, what symbol is used to represent forests? _____

8. Through which continents does the Tropic of Capricorn pass, and on which Atlas map would you look to find it? _____
_____

Thinking Further: What information can you learn more quickly from an atlas than from a gazetteer? Write your answer on a separate sheet.

Atlas, pages 610–629

NAME _____

LEARNING ABOUT SKILLBUILDERS

HIGHLIGHTING SKILLBUILDERS

After each unit in your textbook, two Skillbuilders are presented. The first one helps you practice a social studies skill, such as reading graphs or comparing maps. The second teaches a language arts skill, such as selecting resources or making comparisons. Learning these skills will help you get the most from your textbook.

✳ Use the Skillbuilders in your textbook to answer the questions below.

1. Each Skillbuilder has four parts. Look at the Skillbuilder on pages 278–279. What are the four parts? _____
_____

2. What skill is being taught on pages 606–607, and why do you need it? _____
_____

3. What kinds of graphs are pictured in the Skillbuilder on pages 148–149? _____
_____

4. Look at the two Skillbuilders after Unit 5, on pages 498–501. What is the social studies Skillbuilder, and what is the language arts Skillbuilder for that unit? _____
_____

5. Look at the table in the Skillbuilder on pages 278–279. What three steps are involved in using SQR? _____
_____

6. Look at the Skillbuilder on pages 498–499. What skill is being taught, and why do you need it? _____
_____

7. Look at the Skillbuilder on pages 568–569. How are you asked to practice the skill of making predictions? _____
_____

Thinking Further: One Skillbuilder in your textbook teaches selecting resources. Without reading the Skillbuilder pages, write why you need this skill.

_____
_____
_____

Skillbuilders

NAME _____

WHAT DO ILLUSTRATIONS SHOW?

USING ILLUSTRATIONS

Your textbook contains many different kinds of illustrations, including graphs, diagrams, product charts, time lines, photographs, and reproductions of fine art.

Graphs are drawings that allow you to compare facts. They include line graphs, bar graphs, pie graphs, and pictographs. Diagrams explain how something works or why something happens. Product charts let you see some of the important products made from natural resources, farm crops, and livestock. Time lines show at a glance when events took place. Photographs and pieces of fine art show many things about the time period in which the painting was created or the photograph was taken. By using these and other visual aids in your book, you can "see" facts in a clear way.

✱ Use the illustrations in your textbook to answer the questions below.

1. Look at the time line about the world at war on page 238. During what years was World War I fought? _____

2. Look at the diagram on page 525. What is the fourth step in the silk-producing process? _____

3. Look at the bar graph about rivers in Africa on page 441. Which river is the second longest in Africa? _____

4. Look at the product chart on page 368. Besides date palm fruit and cooking oil, what are three products made from the date palm tree? _____

5. Look at the diagram on page 207. What is the purpose of the cotton gin? _____

6. Look at the photograph of an ancient Roman aqueduct on page 122. What can this photo tell you about the Roman civilization? _____

Thinking Further: Look again at the diagram of the cotton gin on page 207. How is this drawing different from a photograph of this machine?

_____

Illustrations

NAME _____

How Can I Use Special Features?

USING SPECIAL FEATURES

Within the chapters of your textbook are three types of special features. These features are presented to enhance your understanding of the subjects in your textbook.

Features called Using Source Material present important original records as well as secondhand accounts of historical events. These sources provide insight into topics you are studying. Such sources include sayings, historical documents, and transcripts.

Literature features provide excerpts from fiction, such as novels and short stories, and nonfiction, such as diaries and letters. These literature excerpts relate to the topics covered in the chapters in which the excerpts appear.

Features called Citizenship and American Values help you think about social and political issues.

✻ Use the special features in your textbook to answer the questions below.

1. Look at the special feature on page 456. Which of the three types of features is presented there? _____

2. Look at the Literature feature on page 108. Who wrote the play *Julius Caesar*, and where is it set? _____

3. What original document is excerpted on page 380? _____

4. Look at the Citizenship and American Values special feature on pages 82–83. What is the topic of this feature? _____

5. Look at the Literature feature on page 176. Who is the author, and when and where does the story take place? _____
   _____

6. Look at the Using Source Material feature on page 595. Whose journal is being excerpted? _____

7. The Citizenship and American Values feature on pages 548–549 asks you to decide about people's rights to demonstrate against their government. What two opposing views are presented? _____
   _____

Thinking Further: Why is it valuable to read original source material when studying history?

_____
_____

10   Special Features

NAME _____

UNDERSTANDING ROTATION AND REVOLUTION

MAP SKILLS HANDBOOK

✱ The diagram below shows how the tilt of the earth's axis causes the seasons to change. Study the diagram and answer the questions.

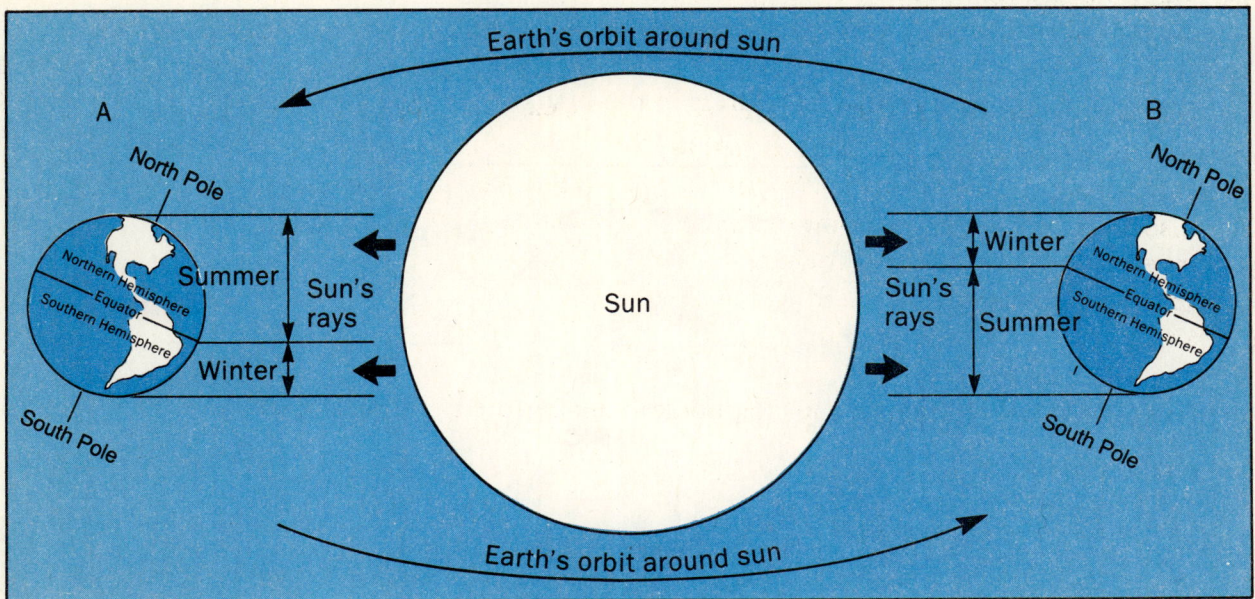

1. Which direction does the earth revolve around the sun, clockwise or counterclockwise? _____

2. When the North Pole is tilted toward the sun, in which hemisphere is it winter? _____

3. Which hemisphere is closer to the sun when it is summer in the Northern Hemisphere? _____

4. Why is it warmer in winter at a place near the Equator than in summer at the North Pole? _____

5. Which month of the year does globe A represent, June or December? _____

6. Which month does globe B represent, June or December? _____

7. When it is summer in the Southern Hemisphere, at which pole does the sun always shine? _____

Thinking Further: Write a paragraph explaining how the temperatures in winter and summer would change if the earth was tilted even more on its axis. Use a separate sheet.

Map Skills Handbook, pages 4–6

NAME _____

IDENTIFYING CITIES BY GLOBAL ADDRESS

MAP SKILLS HANDBOOK

✳ The lines of latitude and longitude on the world map may be used to locate places, just as the signs at cross streets in a town help to locate addresses.
  a. Locate and circle the following lines of latitude and longitude on the map below: 120°W, 80°W, 80°E, 120°E, 160°E, 60°N, 40°N, 20°S, 40°S.
  b. Find each global address listed below on the world map. Write the name of the city located at that address in the blank.

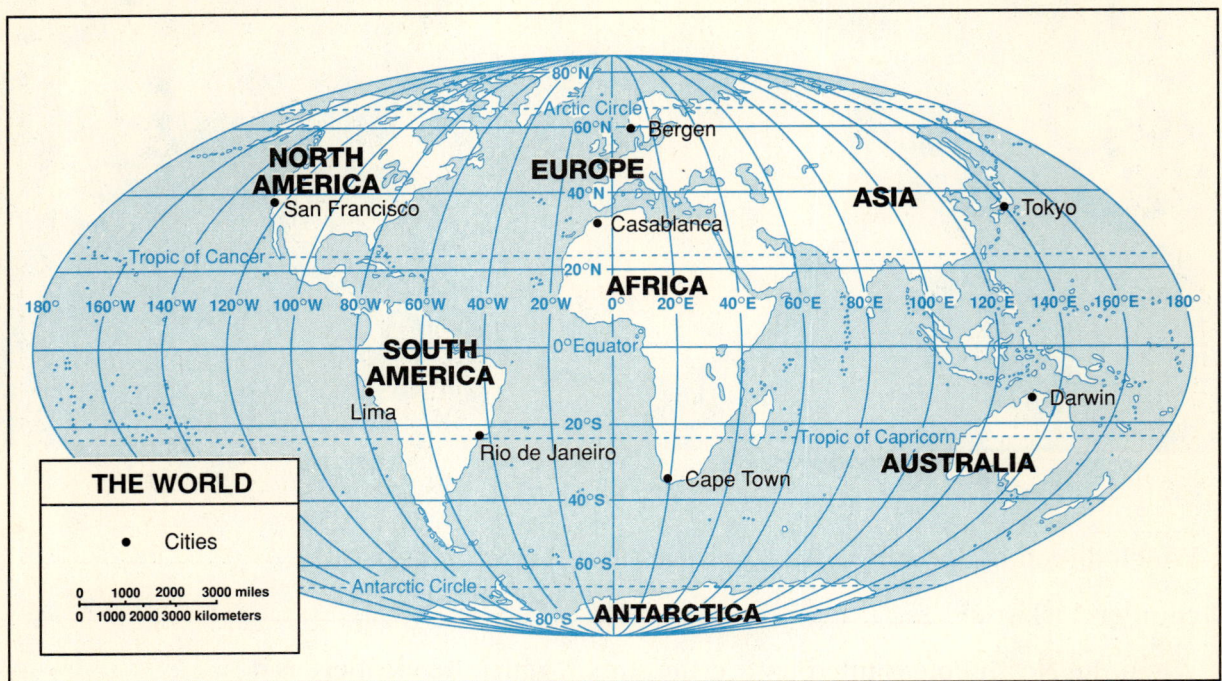

1. 23°S/43°W _____
2. 36°N/140°E _____
3. 60°N/6°E _____
4. 12°S/131°E _____

5. 33°S/19°E _____
6. 33°N/8°W _____
7. 38°N/122°W _____
8. 12°S/77°W _____

Thinking Further: Explain why the longitude lines on the map are curved.

_____
_____
_____
_____
_____

Map Skills Handbook, pages 7–10

NAME _____

SHOWING THE HEIGHT OF THE LAND

MAP SKILLS HANDBOOK

* The map below uses contour lines to show the elevation of the land on two islands, Alpha and Beta.
  a. Using colored pencils or markers, fill in each lettered box on the map key with a different color.
  b. Color the islands, using the correct color for each elevation range.

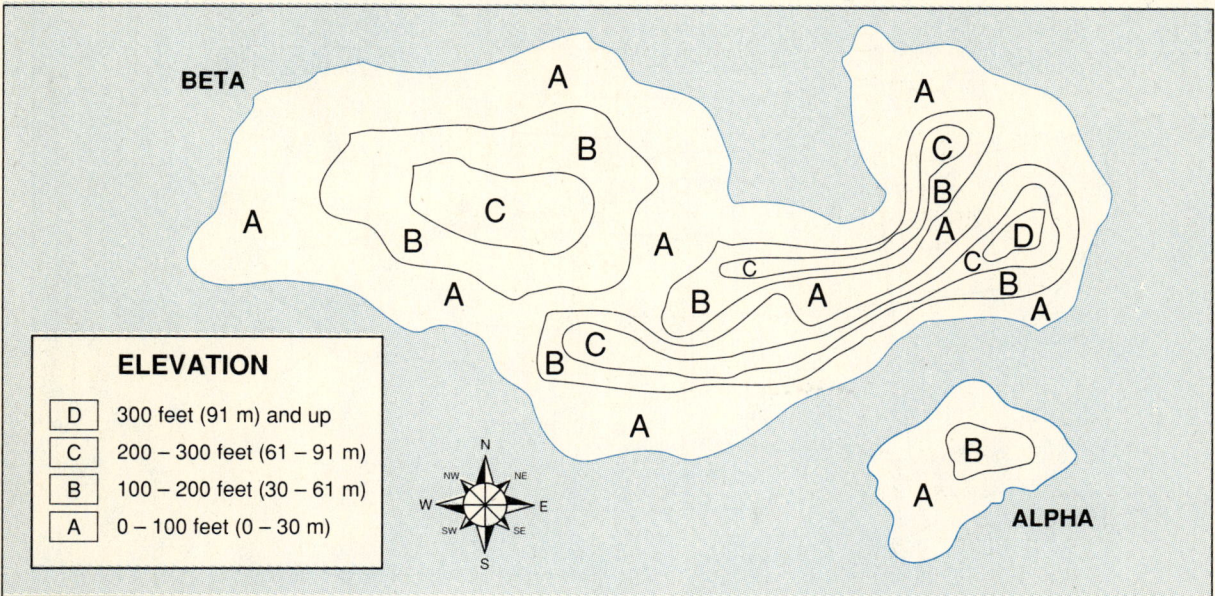

* Fill in each blank with the correct elevation range.

1. The elevation of land along the coast of Alpha and Beta: _____
2. The highest elevation in the western half of Beta: _____
3. The elevation of the valley on Beta: _____
4. The highest elevation on Beta: _____
5. The highest elevation on Alpha: _____
6. The elevation found in only one area of Beta: _____

Thinking Further: Write a paragraph describing some patterns you could use for your map key if you did not have color to show elevations.

_____
_____
_____
_____

NAME _____

FINDING DISTANCE ON A MAP

MAP SKILLS HANDBOOK

✱ School bands from different states traveled to New York City to march in the Thanksgiving Day parade. Using the distance scale on the map below, estimate how far each band had to travel to reach New York.

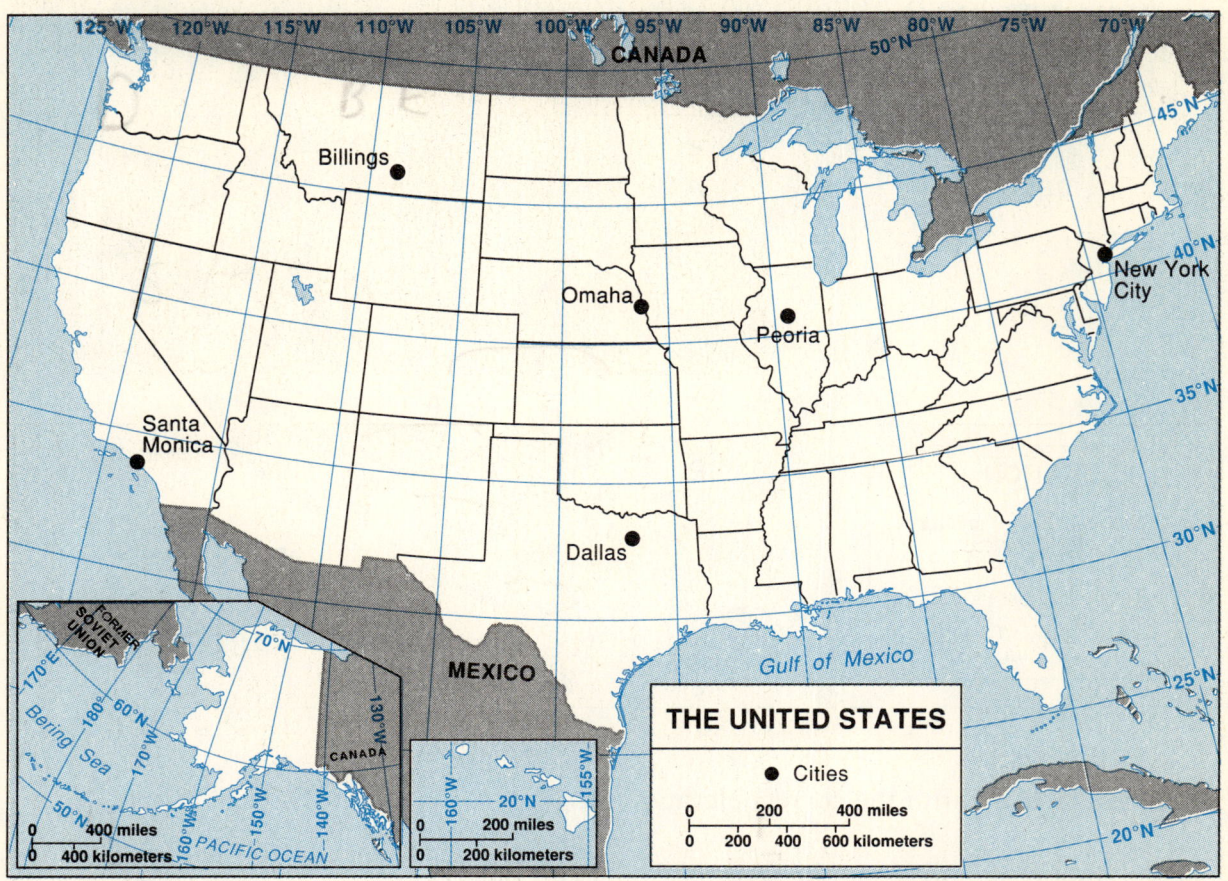

City	Approximate Distance to New York	
	Miles	*Kilometers*
1. Omaha, Nebraska	_____	_____
2. Peoria, Illinois	_____	_____
3. Billings, Montana	_____	_____
4. Santa Monica, California	_____	_____
5. Dallas, Texas	_____	_____

Thinking Further: How big is the mainland United States? Use the distance scale to measure about how many miles it is across the United States from north to south and from east to west.

_____

_____

NAME _____

COMPARING A PHOTOGRAPH AND A MAP

MAP SKILLS HANDBOOK

* Cartographers often draw maps using photographs taken from above the earth. Mapmakers use symbols to represent features in the photograph. The map below was drawn from the aerial photograph shown on the right. Study the photograph and map carefully to see how they are alike and different. Then answer the questions that follow.

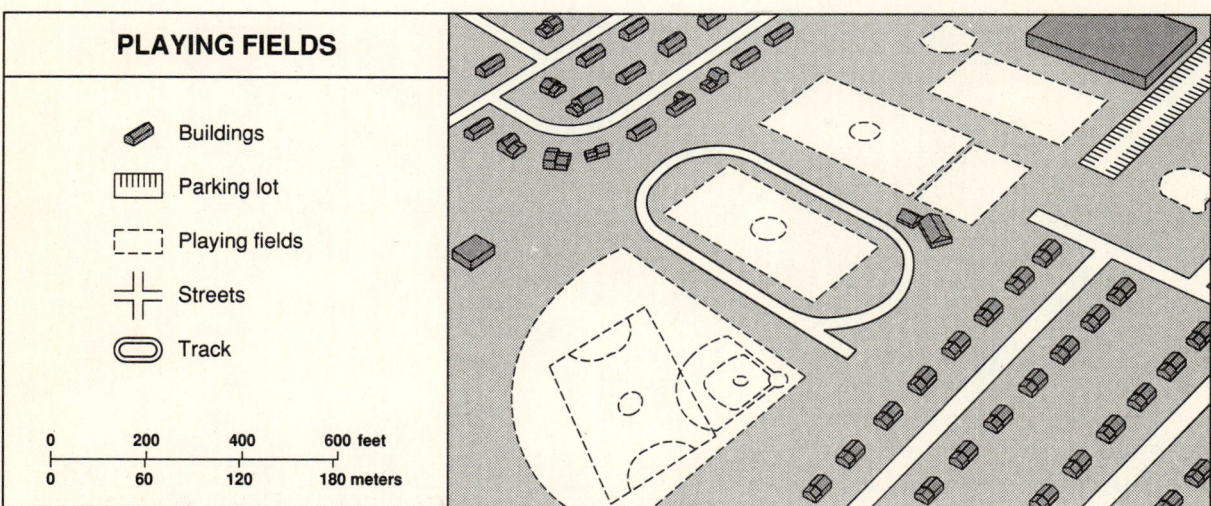

1. How are the map and the photograph alike? _____
2. How are the map and the photograph different? _____
   _____
3. Which is more useful for finding a location? _____
4. List four things you can see on the photograph that do not appear on the map. _____
5. Was the photograph taken from directly above the playing fields? _____

Thinking Further: Trace one of the circles shown on the photograph onto another piece of paper. Explain why the circle is not really round. You may use a separate sheet.

NAME _____

LEARNING ABOUT POLAR PROJECTIONS

MAP SKILLS HANDBOOK

✱ The map below shows a polar projection of the earth. Study the map; then fill in the blanks in the paragraph.

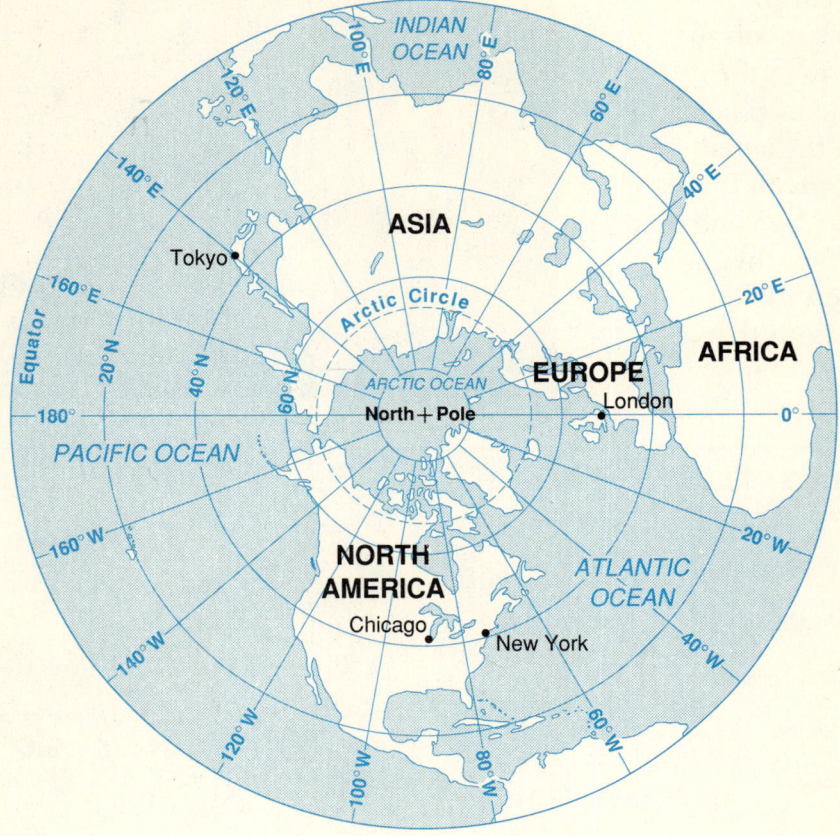

This map shows a polar projection of the _____ Hemisphere, with the _____ Pole at its center. The outer boundary of this map is the _____ latitude line, or the _____. While these maps show only 90° of latitude, they show _____ of longitude. The hemisphere shown on this map includes all of the continents of _____, _____, and _____, and about half of the continent of _____. You can see that an airplane flying the most direct route from New York to Tokyo would cross the Arctic _____ two times.

Thinking Further: Write a paragraph explaining which polar projection would show the part of the earth where most of the earth's people live.

_____

_____

16   Map Skills Handbook, pages 19–21

NAME _____

LOOKING AT PRECIPITATION

MAP SKILLS HANDBOOK

✱ The map below shows the average annual amount of precipitation in Australia. Almost all of the precipitation is rain. Study the map; then answer the questions.

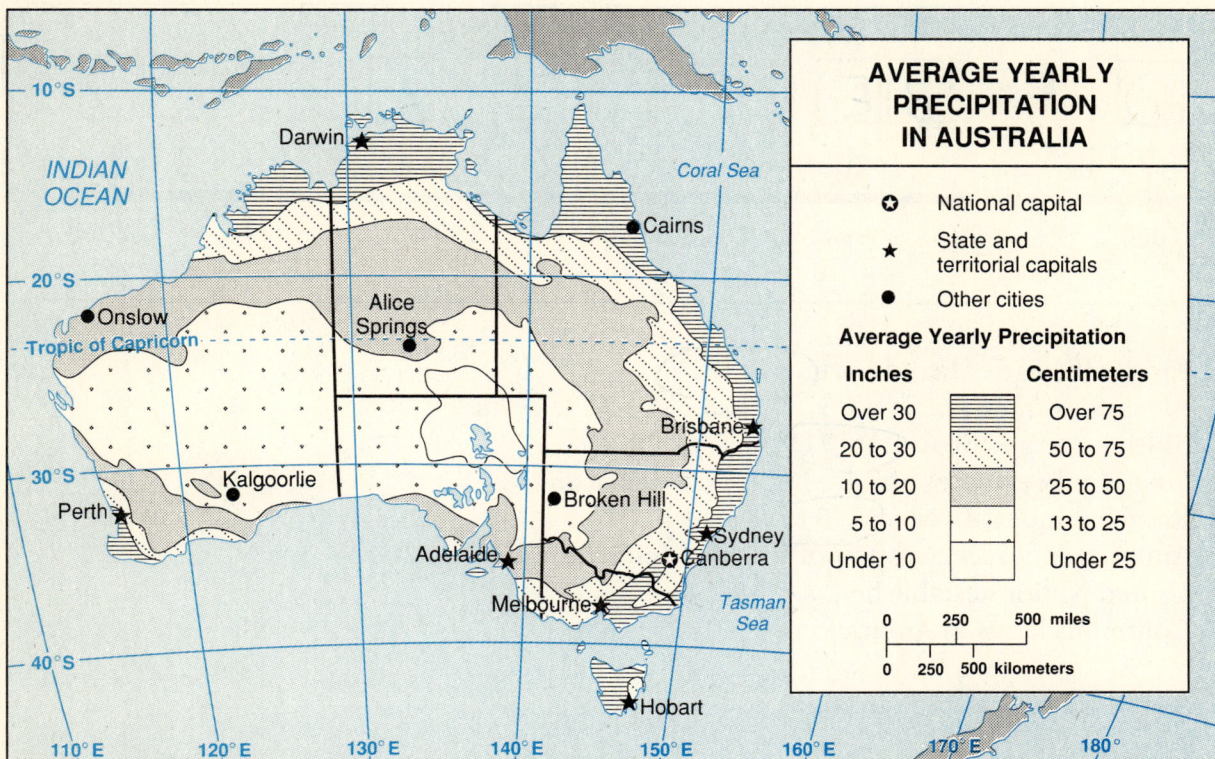

1. Which areas of Australia receive most of the rainfall? _____

2. What pattern do you see in the amounts of precipitation in different areas of Australia? _____

3. Which city receives the most rainfall, Adelaide, Brisbane, or Kalgoorlie? _____

4. What type of climate does the central region of Australia have? _____

5. Does most of Australia receive more than 20 inches or less than 20 inches of precipitation each year? _____

6. On average, how much precipitation does Darwin receive? _____

Thinking Further: Explain why most Australians live in the southeastern part of the country.

_____

Map Skills Handbook, pages 22–25

17

NAME _____

PLACING EVENTS ON A TIME LINE

MAP SKILLS HANDBOOK

✱ The time line below covers the period from 1000 B.C. to A.D. 2000. Put the letter of each event listed in the correct box on the time line.

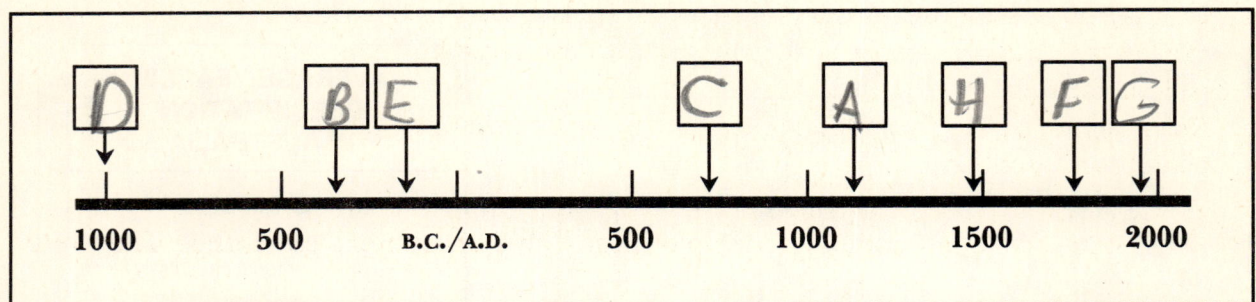

A. King John signs Magna Carta: A.D. 1215
B. Alexander the Great is born: 356 B.C.
C. Muslims invade Spain: A.D. 711
D. First Hindu states established in India: 1000 B.C.
E. Rome conquers Greece: 146 B.C.
F. America issues Declaration of Independence: A.D. 1776
G. United Nations established: A.D. 1945
H. Columbus lands in America: A.D. 1492

✱ Answer the following questions.

1. Number the four events below in the order they happened.

   __4__ United Nations is established. 1945 AD __1__ Rome conquers Greece.
   __2__ Muslims invade Spain. __3__ King John signs Magna Carta.

2. In which century did Columbus land in America? __fourteen hundreds__
3. How many years does the time line show? __3,000 years__
4. How many years after Alexander the Great was born did Greece fall to Rome? __210 years__
5. How many years after the first Hindu states were established in India did King John sign the Magna Carta? __2215 years__

Thinking Further: Explain what the letters B.C. and A.D. on the time line stand for.

_____
_____

Hammurabi's Code of Laws

CHAPTER 1

✻ The following paragraph tells about the Code of Laws of King Hammurabi, who ruled Babylon from ca. 1792 B.C. to 1750 B.C. The coded messages below tell more about the law code.

a. In order to decode the messages, first fill in the key. Do this by writing the letter in the paragraph corresponding with each number. The first is done for you.

b. Referring to the key, decode the messages by writing the correct letter above each number.

The code of Hammurabi was made up of nearly three hundred legal listings. They were
  e   3 11   1   7   2   10 9 14   15 12   18

based on Akkadian and Sumerian laws. The laws covered business, family life, government,
        8   6   13 4   5 16

and witchcraft. There was one overriding principle for all laws.
 17

KEY	A	d	e/E	f	g	h	i	K	l	N	o	r	S	t	u	v	w	y
	1	2	3	4	5	6	7	8	9	10	11	12	13	14	15	16	17	18

The overriding principle for Hammurabi's laws was, "**the strong**
                                                      14 6 3 13 14 12 11 10 5
shall not hurt the weak."
 13 6 1 9 9 10 11 14 6 15 12 14 14 6 3 17 3 1 8

The code provided for **Individual rights**
                       7 10 2 7 16 7 2 15 1 9 12 7 5 6 14 13
and the authority of the
 1 10 2 14 6 3 1 15 14 6 11 12 7 14 18 11 4 14 6 3
state.
 13 14 1 14 3

Thinking Further: What is the main principle underlying the laws of the United States? Give an example of the application of this principle.

_____
_____
_____
_____
_____

Chapter 1, pages 47–53

NAME _____

CHAPTER
1

LEARNING ABOUT THE EARLY EGYPTIANS

✻ Read the paragraphs below. Then circle the correct ending to complete the sentences that follow.

The Egyptians built many pyramids. The three largest and most famous are in the desert at Giza, near present-day Cairo. The largest is the Great Pyramid. Today it would cover nearly ten football fields. It is about 450 feet (137 m) high, but before some of the topmost stones were torn away, it rose to 482 feet (147 m).

Although the pyramids at Giza were built between about 2640 and 2500 B.C., scientists continue to make new discoveries about the individuals and the communities of workers involved in constructing them.

Earlier discoveries revealed much about the rulers of Egypt. More recent searches uncovered some information about the workers. A bakery site near the pyramids has been explored, and many clay pots and baking molds have been found. Scientists now believe workers labored in teams of 20 to 50 to drag the huge stones to the site of the pyramids. The stones were pulled with ropes up ramps from canal barges and from quarries. The workers' great pride in their accomplishments was recorded in pictures at the site.

---

1. Work on the pyramids began in about
   3100 B.C.   2640 B.C.   1500 B.C.   A.D. 250

2. The pyramids are at
   Cairo   Memphis   Giza   Athens

3. At present, the height of the Great Pyramid is about
   137 feet   482 feet   250 feet   450 feet

4. Early discoveries at the pyramids gave little information about
   workers   rulers   pharaohs   queens

5. More recent discoveries have been made at the site of a
   church   library   palace   bakery

6. At the recently excavated site, scientists have dug up
   crowns   jewels   wheels   pots

7. People building the large pyramids worked
   alone   in teams   in pairs   in huge groups

8. Workers dragged stones to the site with the aid of
   ropes   oxen   elephants   camels

Thinking Further: The Great Pyramid has lasted for some 4,500 years. Besides the pyramids, what large structures in the world today might last that long? Give a reason or two why you think the structure will be durable. Write your answer on a separate sheet.

NAME _____

CHAPTER 1

EXAMINING THE COURSE OF THE NILE

✱ The Nile River is the world's longest river. It flows about 4,200 miles (about 6,800 km), from Burundi, in East Africa, to northern Egypt. It has several big waterfalls, called cataracts. In addition, the river has many tributaries, some of which are major rivers. Study the map below and answer the questions.

1. In which country is the greatest length of the Nile located? _Egypt_ Which country contains the second greatest length? _____

2. Ruins of ancient Meroe exist today. About how many miles south of the Egyptian border are they?

   _____

3. What is the name of the largest lake in the Nile River System? _____ What is the second largest lake?

   _____

4. If you had the time and energy, could you row a small boat from Lake Victoria to Alexandria without taking it out of the water? Give a reason for your answer.

   _____
   _____

5. Khartoum is a large, bustling city. Does its geographical location suggest one reason why it became important? Why?

   _____
   _____
   _____

Thinking Further: In what ways can a river link people living far apart?

_____
_____
_____

Chapter 1, pages 54–58

NAME _____

CHAPTER **1**

THE GEOGRAPHY OF ANCIENT ISRAEL

✱ Study the map below of the kingdom of David and Solomon. Then fill in the blanks. Refer to a map in your textbook, if necessary.

1. The Mediterranean Sea, which formed part of the western boundary of the kingdom, is called the _____ on this map.

2. Jerusalem was near what is now called the Dead Sea but was once called the Salt Sea.

3. The kingdom of David and Solomon was made up of six territories named _____ _____.

4. To the east of the kingdom was the _____.

5. Israel was bordered on the west by _____, and on the east by _____ and _____.

6. An independent kingdom located west of Judah was _____.

7. The Salt Sea helped divide the territories of _____ and _____.

8. The territory located farthest north was called _____.

9. A major city in Ammon was _____.

10. A major city northwest of Ammon was _____.

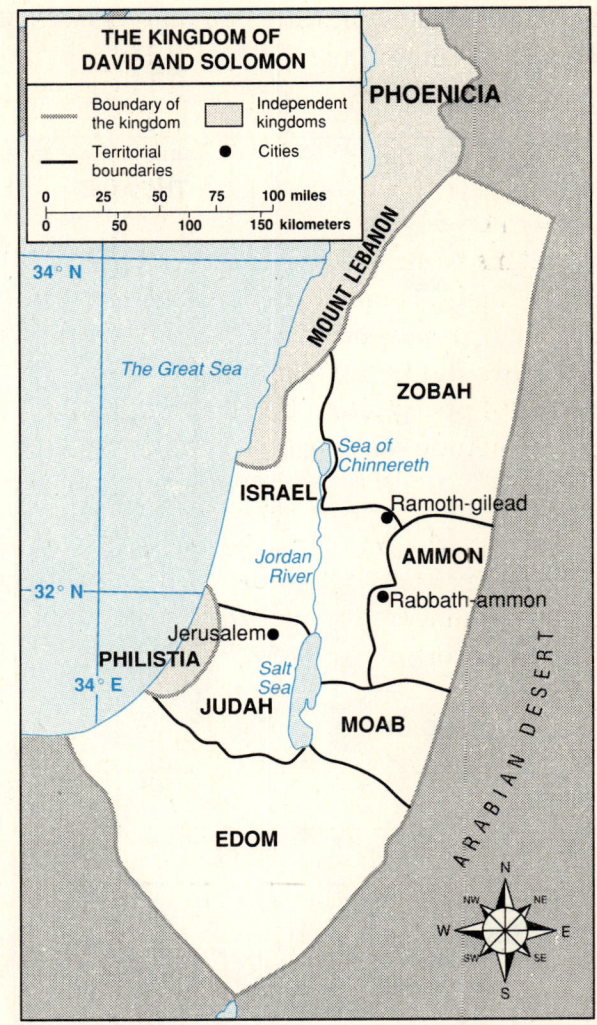

Thinking Further: In ancient kingdoms a person might live in a community that was part of a larger political unit. The same is true today. To what two or three political units does your city or town belong?

_____
_____

NAME ______________________________ **CHAPTER 1**

The Life of King Solomon

✻ A biography tells the story of a person's life. The author of a biography sometimes highlights a person's qualities. The admirable qualities are called strengths while others are considered weaknesses. Read this short biography about Israel's great King Solomon.

Soon after Solomon was made king of Israel, he became known for his great wisdom in judging people. To honor God for all his blessings, Solomon had a great temple built. He wrote wisely about life and observed and reported about the natural world around him. Solomon also wrote beautiful poetry about his love for God. In time Solomon became very wealthy, and with his great wealth he began to be wasteful. He built large ornamental war chariots and bought more and more horses for the huge stables he had constructed. Solomon had many wives, and he built idols to honor the gods of each wife. He taxed his people heavily and made slaves of the people he conquered to advance his building programs.

✻ On the lines that follow, write four strengths and four weaknesses of Solomon that are mentioned in the biography. One strength has been written in for you.

Strengths

1. Solomon wrote poetry.
2. ______________________________
3. ______________________________
4. ______________________________

Weaknesses

1. ______________________________
2. ______________________________
3. ______________________________
4. ______________________________

Thinking Further: Choose someone whom you consider to be great and describe some of his or her strengths and weaknesses.

____

____

____

NAME _____

REMEMBERING PEOPLE

CHAPTER **1**

* Fill in the blanks before the descriptions below with the names of the persons described. All possible names are in the box.

Gilgamesh	Tutankhamen	
David	Hatshepsut	Hammurabi
Saul	Belzoni	Joseph
Goliath	Champollion	

_____ a shepherd who became a king

_____ a treasure hunter who discovered the tomb of Seti I

__Goliath__ a giant who represented the Philistines

_____ the hero of a popular work of Mesopotamian literature discovered in 1850

__Joseph__ a descendant of Abraham who became a high official of a pharaoh

_____ a king of Babylon who ordered that laws be carved on a pillar

_____ the solver of the puzzle of the Rosetta stone

_____ the Egyptian god-king who wore a false beard

__Tutankhamen__ a boy-king who ruled Egypt in the middle of the twelfth century B.C.

_____ the king who led the Israelites against the Philistines

Thinking Further: Which of the ten persons listed in the box above do you think was most important? Give two or three reasons to support your choice.

_____
_____
_____
_____
_____

NAME _____

CHAPTER 2

INTERPRETING A GREEK MYTH

* A myth is a story that explains some custom, belief, or happening in nature. It usually involves gods and goddesses, or other supernatural beings. Read this myth about the Greek goddess Athena. Then answer the questions that follow.

Athena, the goddess of war and wisdom, was the beautiful daughter of Zeus, ruler of the gods. She was generous and skilled, and she shared her knowledge with humans. She showed ordinary people how to make tools and musical instruments, and how to spin wool yarn and make woven cloth.

Athena was sometimes jealous of other gods or of humans who did something better than she. A young woman named Arachne (uh RAK nee) was an excellent weaver. Arachne was fast and neat and her designs were unusual and colorful. Neighboring people came to see the large tapestry (heavy cloth) that she had woven. The tapestry showed the gods Poseidon and Prometheus and the goddess Aphrodite. All this attention made Arachne so proud that she boasted, "I am an even better weaver than Athena. She may have been the master teacher, but look at *my* beautiful work."

When Athena heard this, she went to see Arachne and the tapestry. She saw that it was indeed better than she could have done herself. This made Athena so jealous and angry that she ripped the tapestry apart.

Arachne was very frightened and ran into the woods to escape. However, Athena caught Arachne and transformed her into a spider, saying, "You can still weave, little one. But now your thread will be a thousand times finer and your work a thousand times more delicate."

---

1. Why do you think Athena shared her knowledge with humans? _____
   _____
   _____

2. How did Arachne arouse Athena's anger? _____
   _____

3. Why was Athena so upset when she saw Arachne's tapestry? _____
   _____

4. What Greek city is named in Athena's honor? _____

Thinking Further: Do you think Athena had a right to be upset with Arachne?
_____
_____
_____

Comparing Athens and Sparta

Chapter 2

* The statements below might have been written by citizens of either the city-state of Athens or the city-state of Sparta. On the line before each statement, enter the name of the city-state the writer probably lived in. The first has been done for you.

_____Sparta_____ 1. "My son will be seven years old next month, and he will leave home to become a soldier."

_____ 2. "My brother has been called to serve on a jury next week. My uncle served on a jury last year."

_____ 3. "I have just completed my military service. Now I may marry."

_____ 4. "I enjoyed learning about Pericles' ideas. He describes our government very well."

_____ 5. "Darius and his Persian soldiers attacked us recently. We achieved a great victory over the invaders at Marathon."

_____ 6. "When my friends and I were at the marketplace this morning, we heard many interesting ideas about equality before the law."

_____ 7. "If I do not get married, I will be breaking the law."

_____ 8. "My wife and I were relieved that our baby was born strong and healthy. Now he will be allowed to live."

_____ 9. "You do not have to be born into a wealthy family in order to get ahead. My parents are poor, but I own a successful business."

_____ 10. "I am very happy about Solon's reforms. He canceled my debts, and now I will be able to farm without having to worry about money I owe."

Thinking Further: In two or three sentences tell whether you would have preferred living in ancient Athens or in ancient Sparta. Support your choice with at least two specific reasons.

_____

_____

_____

_____

_____

_____

NAME _____

CHAPTER 2

ALEXANDER THE GREAT

✱ This crossword puzzle is based on information in Lesson 3 of Chapter 2. Use the clues to complete the puzzle.

ACROSS

1. City where Alexander the Great died
2. Country Alexander fought to free Greek cities in Asia
4. Country in north Africa conquered by Alexander
7. Alexander's homeland
9. Person who taught Alexander
11. Alexander's age when he became king (write out number)
12. Alexander's father

DOWN

1. Name of Alexander the Great's horse
2. His house was the only one left standing when Thebes was destroyed by Alexander
3. Name given to many Greek cities in regions Alexander conquered
5. Macedonia was located in the _____ of Greece
6. Settlement of people living in new area while being ruled by government of another country
8. River at far eastern edge of Alexander's empire
10. City destroyed by Alexander to prove he was ready to be king

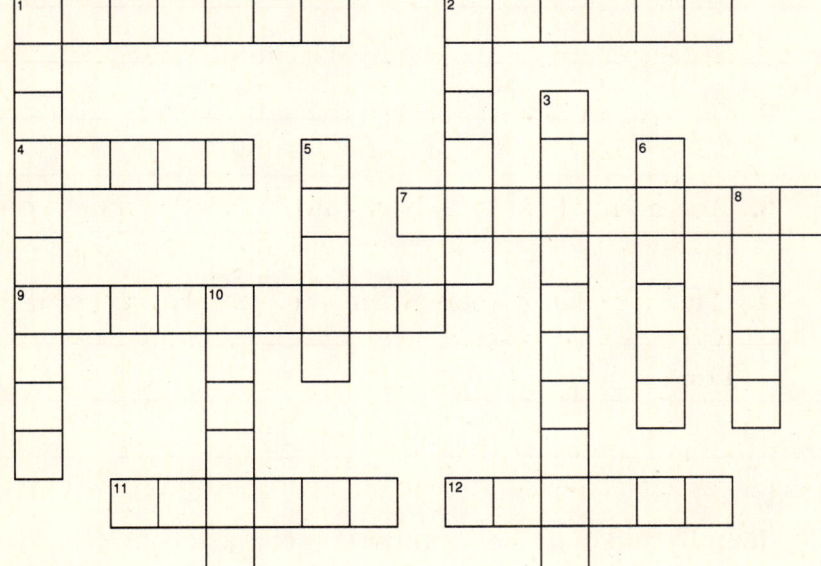

Thinking Further: What do you think is the most important fact about Alexander's career? Give two or three reasons for your choice.

_____
_____
_____

NAME _____

CHAPTER 2

THE GEOGRAPHY OF ANCIENT GREECE

✱ On the facing page is a map of ancient Greece.
a. Locate the following places and geographical features on the map.
b. Write each number in the appropriate spot.
c. On the lines next to each place or geographical feature, give one or two important reasons why it was significant in ancient times. (You may wish to refer to a map in your textbook to help you with this exercise.)

1. Mt. Olympus _____
   _____
   _____
   _____

2. Athens _____
   _____
   _____
   _____

3. Sparta _____
   _____
   _____
   _____

4. Troy _____
   _____
   _____
   _____

5. Salamis _____
   _____
   _____
   _____

6. Thebes _____
   _____
   _____
   _____

7. Macedonia _____
   _____
   _____
   _____

8. Aegean Sea _____
   _____
   _____
   _____

Thinking Further: Identify and describe an important characteristic of the geography of Greece.

_____
_____
_____
_____
_____

NAME _____

The Geography of Ancient Greece CONTINUED

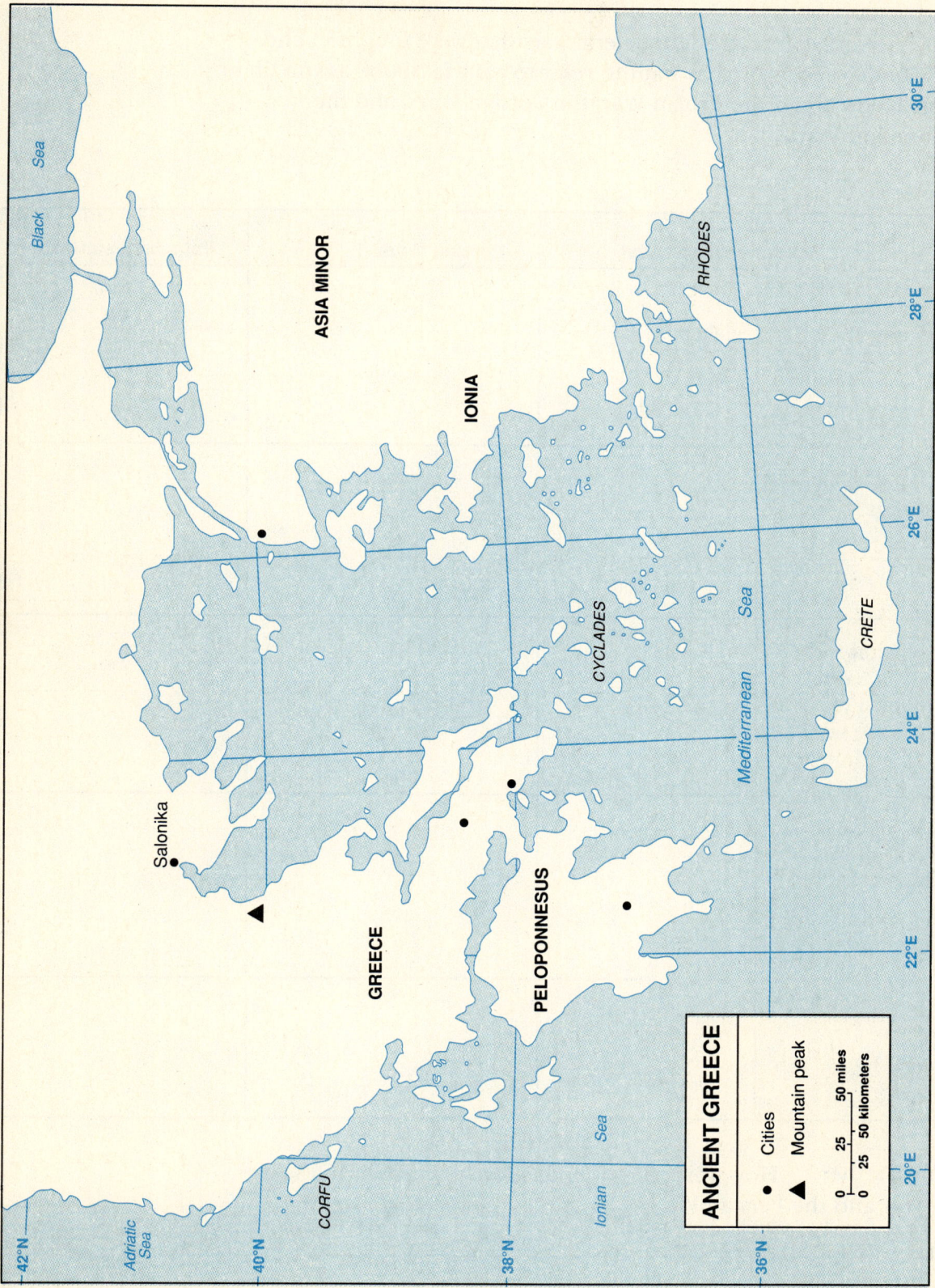

NAME _____

CHAPTER 2

COMPARING ANCIENT WARS

* In Chapter 2 you read about several wars that were fought in and near ancient Greece. You may want to refer to your textbook as you fill in the chart below about the Trojan War, the Persian Wars, and the Peloponnesian War.

	Trojan War	Persian Wars	Peloponnesian War
Who were the combatants?	vs.	vs.	vs.
What caused the war to start?			
What was the main strategy or battle plan that led to victory in the war?			
Why do you think this strategy was effective?			
Who won the war?			

Thinking Further: How were the winning strategies similar in the Trojan War and the Persian Wars?

_____

_____

_____

NAME _____

CHAPTER 3

COMPARING GOVERNMENTS

* The United States is a republic. In a republic citizens choose representatives to run the country. The government of the United States resembles and differs from that of the ancient Roman Republic. In the chart below, basic information about the two governments is listed in categories. Fill in the missing information.

	Roman Republic	**United States Today**
Equality of citizens	Citizens were divided into two unequal groups, patricians and plebeians.	With few exceptions, such as some convicted criminals, all citizens are equal.
Voting rights		With few exceptions, all citizens 18 years old and older can vote.
Qualifications for senator	Only patricians could become senators.	
Title of chief executive and length of term		
Number of chief executives at one time		
Government during major emergency		The President continues to lead during emergencies, no matter how serious.

Thinking Further: Did average citizens play a larger role in the government of the ancient Roman Republic, compared to citizens in the United States today? Support your answer with specific reasons.

_____
_____
_____

NAME _____

CHAPTER
3

ROMULUS AND REMUS

✱   Historians know little about the founding of the city of Rome. According to myth, the city was founded by twin brothers, Romulus and Remus. The passage below tells one version of their story. (A myth explains something about the world, usually by referring to gods or other supernatural beings.)

According to myth, twin boys were born to a priestess named Rhea Silvia. The father of the babies was Mars, the Roman god of war. When the king of the region heard of the babies' birth, he ordered them thrown into the Tiber River because he feared the god Mars. The babies were put into a basket and thrown into the river. However, the basket was washed ashore and became tangled in the roots of a large tree on a riverbank. Mars sent a wolf to care for the twins. A poor herdsman found the babies in the wolf's den and took them home to raise. He named them Romulus and Remus.

Many years later, the twins, now grown, were reunited with their grandfather, a king named Numitor. After living with Numitor for several years, Romulus and Remus yearned for power. They set out to establish a new settlement on the banks of the Tiber River where they had been found by the wolf. After working together to start the new city, the twins began to fight about which of them should rule. The strife ended when Romulus flew into a rage and killed his brother. The people of the new city accepted Romulus as their king. The city came to be called Rome after its ruler.

✱   Rank the following events according to the order in which they take place in the myth. (Use the numbers 1 to 8.)

_____   Twin sons are born to Rhea Silvia.

_____   Romulus and Remus are reunited with their grandfather.

_____   A city is named Rome after its leader.

_____   Mars sends a wolf to care for the babies.

_____   Romulus and Remus set off to start a new city.

_____   A herdsman finds the babies in a wolf's den.

_____   Remus is killed by his brother.

_____   The babies are thrown into the Tiber River.

Thinking Further: You have just read a myth about the founding of Rome. Describe a more realistic way in which Rome might have been founded.

_____

_____

INTERPRETING A MAP OF ANCIENT BRITAIN

CHAPTER 3

✻ In 55 B.C., the Roman conqueror Julius Caesar landed in Britain to prevent the British from helping the Gauls, who were at war with Rome. Caesar returned to Britain the following year, but he never conquered it. A century later, portions of the island were seized by the Roman emperor Claudius I. By A.D. 85, Rome possessed most of Britain. The map shows Britain in A.D. 85. Study the map, and then answer each question by writing the letter of the correct choice in the blank.

__C__ 1. Which of the cities below is farthest west?
   a. Eburacum   c. Isca
   b. Lindum   d. Deva

_____ 2. In which direction should you travel to get from Londinium to the Wall of Hadrian?
   a. north   c. south
   b. east   d. west

_____ 3. Where is the Wall of Antoninus?
   a. north of Deva   c. west of Isca
   b. west of Ireland   d. east of Lindum

_____ 4. Which of the following cities is closest to the North Sea?
   a. Isca   c. Eburacum
   b. Deva   d. Cassiterides

_____ 5. About how far is it from Camulodunum to Eburacum?
   a. 100 miles   c. 225 miles
   b. 175 miles   d. 300 miles

_____ 6. Which ancient British town is nearest Ireland?
   a. Cassiterides   c. Deva
   b. Lindum   d. Eburacum

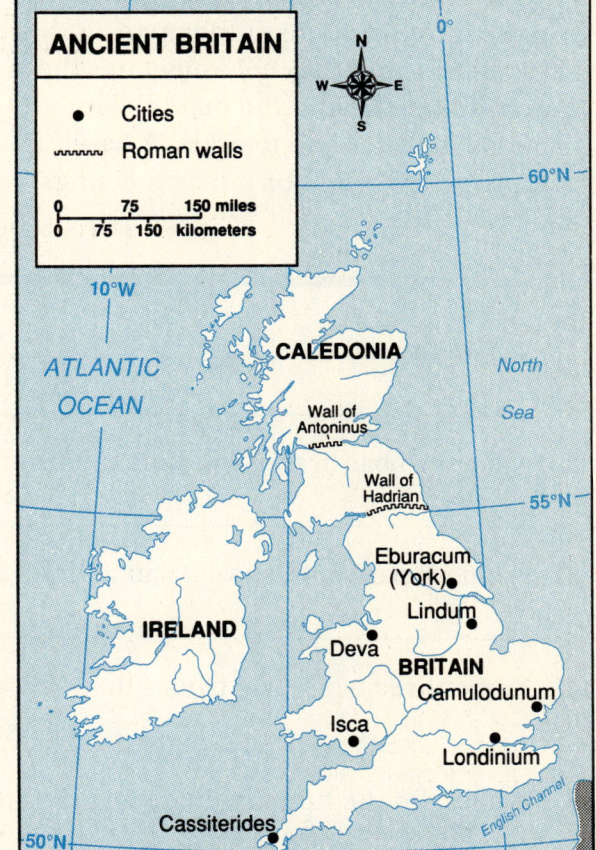

_____ 7. Which ancient British town is closest to the Prime Meridian (0° longitude)?
   a. Isca   c. Londinium
   b. Deva   d. Eburacum

Thinking Further: Discuss at least two major differences in geography between ancient Britain and modern Great Britain.

_____

_____

NAME _____

THE ROMAN FORUM

CHAPTER **3**

✱ On the facing page is an illustration of part of the Roman Forum in early times. The following paragraphs give some background information. Use the illustration and the paragraphs to answer the questions below.

The Roman Forum was the main center of public life. People met friends at the forum and kept up with the news. They bought and sold goods at the open-air marketplace, and they held meetings there. The buildings around the marketplace included basilicas and temples. A basilica was a large hall used for public meetings and law courts.

The Romans worshiped many gods. They even made gods of their dead heroes. Each god had his or her own temple, and many of these temples were clustered around the forum. A forum also included other structures that related to public life, such as arches and statues built to commemorate heroes and great events.

---

1. What is a basilica? _____
   _____

2. Name two basilicas in the Roman Forum. _____
   _____

3. From where would a politician address an outdoor meeting? _____
   _____

4. Name three types of activities that took place at a forum. _____
   _____

5. Where did the Roman senate meet? _____
   _____

6. Why, do you think, were there forums in the towns the Romans built in Britain and other provinces? _____
   _____

Thinking Further: Think of a major government or religious building in your community. In what specific ways is its appearance similar to, or different from, a comparable building in a Roman forum?
_____
_____
_____

NAME _____

CHAPTER 3

The Roman Forum CONTINUED

EXPLORING THE ROMAN FORUM

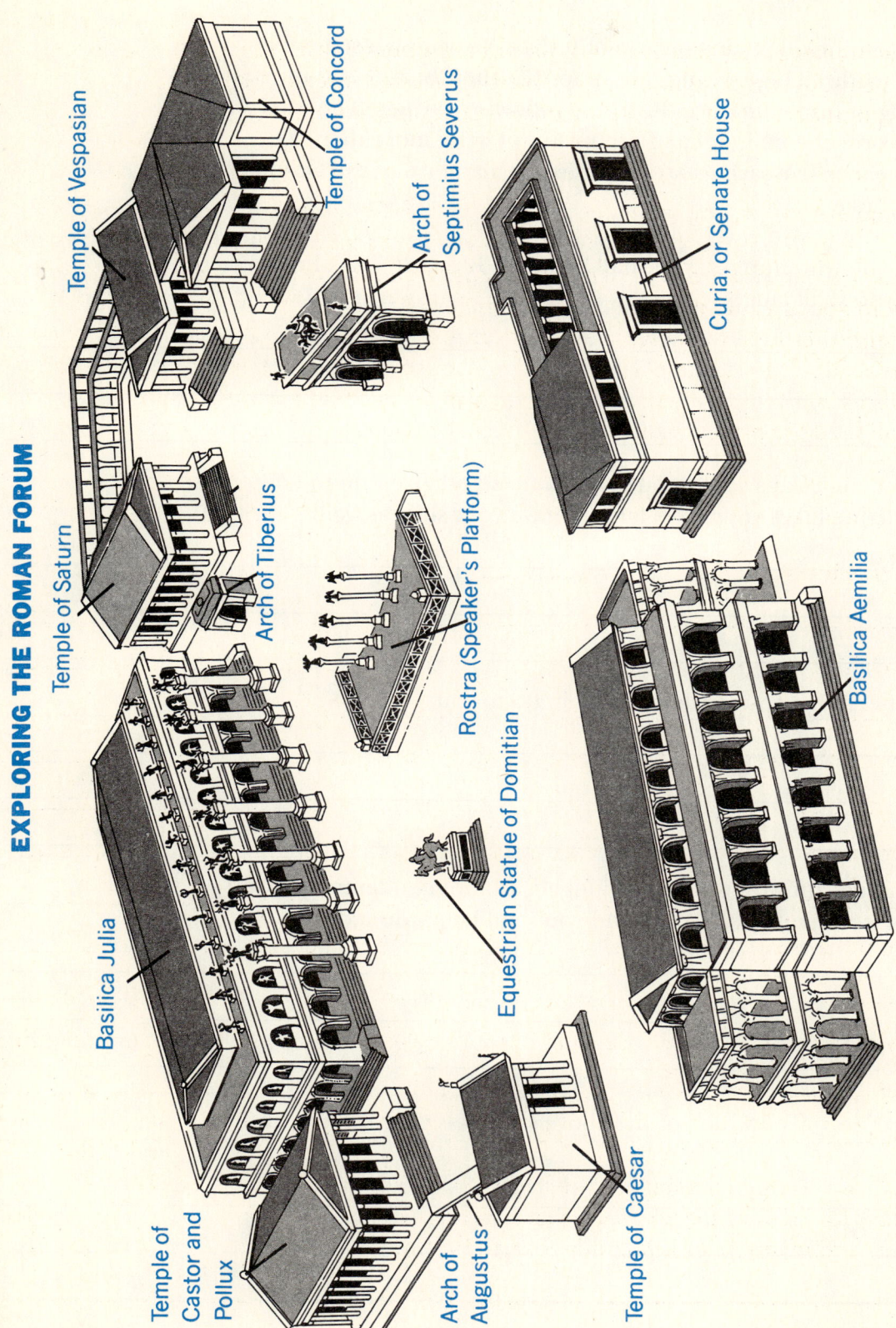

Chapter 3, pages 112–115

NAME _____

CHAPTER 3

THE SAYINGS OF JESUS

✱ The Gospels include many sayings of Jesus. (A saying is a statement of wisdom or truth.) These sayings are noted for their beauty and their understanding of human nature. Read the following sayings. Then tell in your own words the main idea of each. Do not write more than two sentences for each. The sayings are taken from Chapter 6 of the Gospel According to Luke.

1. "Blest are you who hunger; you shall be filled. Blest are you who are weeping; you shall laugh."

   _____
   _____
   _____

2. "When someone slaps you on one cheek, turn and give him the other; when someone takes your coat, let him have your shirt as well."

   _____
   _____
   _____

3. "Do to others what you would have them do to you."

   _____
   _____
   _____

4. "Do not judge, and you will not be judged. Do not condemn, and you will not be condemned. Pardon, and you shall be pardoned."

   _____
   _____
   _____

Thinking Further: Tell which of the above sayings is your favorite and explain why.

_____
_____
_____
_____

NAME _____

LATIN INFLUENCE ON ENGLISH

CHAPTER 3

* Each sentence below contains one Latin word, printed in italic type. On the line, write an English word that comes from the Latin word. The English word should make sense in the sentence.

_____ 1. Not all children living in ancient Rome attended a *schola*.

_____ 2. Marc thought Julia's rude behavior was *inexcusabilis*.

_____ 3. After you *addera* the numerals, write down the total.

_____ 4. Many buildings in the Roman Forum were known for their *elegantia*.

_____ 5. *Musica* and theater were important to the Romans.

_____ 6. Hannibal was able to *supervivere* in the Alps because he came well prepared.

_____ 7. A pat on the back can be a *comfortare* when you're feeling sad.

_____ 8. A Roman *captivus* found his cell was dark and often damp.

Thinking Further: Many English prefixes come from Latin. (A prefix is a syllable or word placed at the beginning of another word or root to change its meaning or to create a new word.) Below are three English prefixes that come from Latin. The meaning of each prefix is in parentheses. Write two English words that begin with each prefix. Write a sentence for each word.

bi- (two)

_____
_____

in- (not)

_____
_____

re- (again)

_____
_____

Chapter 3, pages 120–123

NAME _____

CHAPTER 4

THINKING LIKE AN ARCHAEOLOGIST

* Archaeology is the scientific study of the materials of ancient civilizations. Such materials include buildings, pottery, and tools. An archaeologist is one who searches for and studies the materials to determine what life was like in the past. Archaeologists at the Harappa and Mohenjo-Daro sites uncovered a great deal of information about life in ancient India and Pakistan.

Imagine it is the year A.D. 3020. A team of archaeologists is conducting a "dig" in the remains of the community where you lived. What types of items might the archaeologists uncover to help them understand what life was like in the 1990s? Remember that an item must be very hard and strong to last for more than 1,000 years. For example, wood and cloth made in 1990 would probably disintegrate long before 3020. On the other hand, most metals and bricks can last for many centuries. Write at least two examples next to each type of item in the list below. Two items have already been listed for you.

Type of Item	Examples
Home life	Microwave oven, _____
Clothing	_____
Transportation	_____
Communications	Television set, _____
Art	_____
Recreation	_____

Thinking Further: Archaeologists study the ancient past. Their work has little direct connection with our day-to-day life. Do you think archaeology nevertheless is important for all of us? Support your answer with two or three specific reasons.

_____
_____
_____
_____

NAME _____

CHAPTER 4

COMPARING THE BUDDHA AND ASOKA

✻ Each statement below describes either the Buddha or Emperor Asoka. Write either **B**, for the Buddha, or **A**, for Emperor Asoka, in the blanks on the left.

_____ 1. His name means "the enlightened one."

_____ 2. He was a powerful ruler who decided that war and suffering were wrong.

_____ 3. He lived in caves to try to find a more satisfying way of life.

_____ 4. He erected stone pillars with Buddhist teachings carved on them.

_____ 5. He sent religious teachers to Alexandria and perhaps to China.

_____ 6. When he was growing up, he was not allowed to see or hear anything unpleasant.

_____ 7. He planted trees and dug wells to make travel in his kingdom more comfortable.

_____ 8. He was the son of a king who ruled part of what is now India and Nepal.

_____ 9. He believed that a truly wise person is an unselfish person.

_____ 10. He lived in the third century B.C.

_____ 11. He got his name from his students.

_____ 12. According to legend, his children planted a bo tree in Sri Lanka.

_____ 13. He was influenced by the sight of an ascetic.

Thinking Further: According to legend, Siddhartha Gautama's life might have taken him in either of two directions. He could have become a powerful king or a great teacher of wisdom. He took the second direction and eventually became the Buddha. Tell whether you think Siddhartha took the right course. Give two or three reasons to support your opinion.

_____
_____
_____
_____
_____

NAME _____

CHAPTER 4

EARLY CHINESE CIVILIZATION

✱ The following statements might have been spoken by great figures in ancient China. Write the name of the likely speaker in the blank following each statement. A speaker may have uttered more than one statement.

1. "I showed the Chinese people the advantage of trade." _____
2. "I taught the Chinese people to respect all religions." _____
3. "I made sure that all Chinese used the same kind of money." _____
4. "I was alive at the same time as the Buddha." _____
5. "I had the people build an army of clay soldiers to protect my tomb." _____

Thinking Further: Here are some sayings that probably originated with Confucius and his followers. On the lines following each saying tell *in your own words* what the saying means. Then tell whether you agree or disagree with the saying. Do not write more than three sentences for any saying.

1. "When you have faults, do not fear to abandon them." _____
_____
_____
_____

2. "To go beyond is as wrong as to fall short." _____
_____
_____
_____

3. "The superior man is modest in his speech, but surpasses in his actions." _____
_____
_____
_____

4. "What you do not want done to yourself, do not do to others." _____
_____
_____
_____

NAME _____

CHAPTER 4

Chinese Culture

✱ Read the following paragraph about the importance of writing in China since ancient times. Then complete each sentence in Column 2 below by writing in the correct word(s) from Column 1.

Writing and painting have been a part of Chinese life for many centuries. Many Chinese consider fine writing to be a part of painting. The same brush is used for both, and a painting and a poem are often prepared as one piece of art. The Chinese expect all writing to be expressed in beautiful language. This writing includes works about science, history, religion, and politics as well as poetry. The people chosen for government service have been highly honored in China. Government officers have long had to pass tests to obtain a post. The most important parts of these tests require candidates to demonstrate their ability to compose poetry or prose.

Column 1

government service

write and paint

many centuries

test

beautiful language

compose poetry and prose

one piece of art

science, history, religion, and politics

Column 2

1. To become government officials Chinese people have to show their ability to _____.

2. Writing and painting have been important in China for _____.

3. Writing and painting are often prepared together as _____.

4. People in China have been highly honored when chosen for _____.

5. Writers of science and history are expected to use _____.

6. Besides poetry, subjects of good writing are _____.

7. One brush is used to _____.

8. To obtain a government post the Chinese have to pass a _____.

Thinking Further: Do you think poetry and painting are similar to one another, or are they quite different? Give specific reasons for your answer. Write your answer on a separate sheet.

NAME _____

CHAPTER 4

INTERPRETING A MAP

✱ Below are products and symbols to represent them and a map of part of the Indian subcontinent. The map depicts the upper Indus River System of modern Pakistan. Refer to the products list and map to answer the questions.

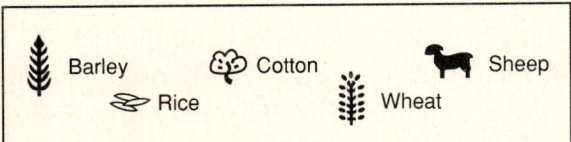

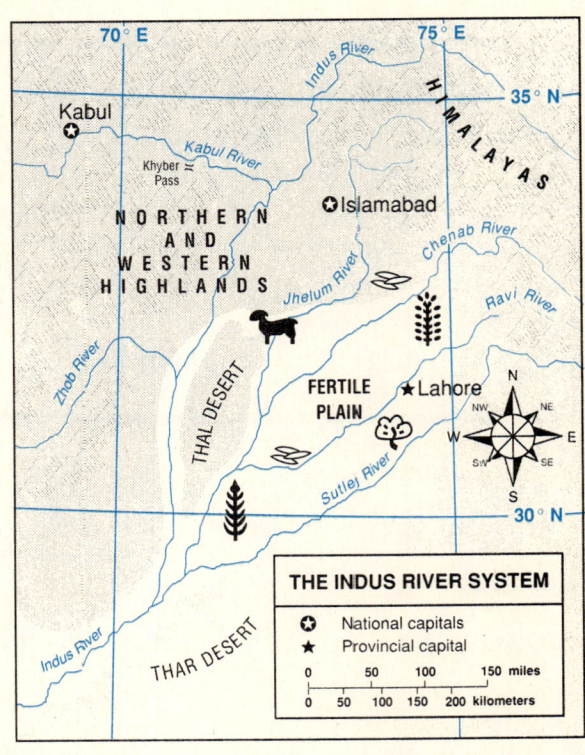

1. In which area on the map do you think large numbers of people might have settled long ago? Give a reason for your answer. _____
_____
_____

2. Why would people be less likely to settle in the area south of the fertile plain?
_____
_____
_____

3. How might people reach Islamabad by land from Kabul?
_____
_____
_____

4. In which direction does the Indus River System probably flow?
_____
_____
_____

5. Name two reasons why a river system can be important to a region such as the fertile plain. _____
_____
_____

6. According to the map, which of the products listed above are raised in the fertile plain? _____
_____
_____

Thinking Further: A limited number of items are produced in the fertile plain. What basic products would people of the region need to import, or bring in? In two or three sentences name a few imports and tell why they would be needed.

_____
_____
_____

NAME _____

CHAPTER 4

UNDERSTANDING KEY FACTS ABOUT BELIEFS

✳ Use the information in the table to help answer the questions below. (Islam is not included in the table because it was founded much later than the belief systems listed.)

Early Religions and Philosophies

Belief System	Region Where Founded	Time Founded	Traditional Founder	Major Holy Writings
Judaism	Middle East	ca. 1700 B.C.	Abraham	Torah
Hinduism	India	ca. 1500 B.C.	[no single founder]	Vedas
Buddhism	India	ca. 500 B.C.	Siddhartha Gautama	Tripitika
Confucianism	China	ca. 500 B.C.	Confucius	Five Classics
Christianity	Middle East	ca. A.D. 30	Jesus	Bible

1. In what order do the belief systems appear on the table? _____
2. In what other logical order might the table be arranged? _____
3. What does the abbreviation *ca.* stand for? _____ What does this word mean? _____
4. Over approximately how many years were the five belief systems founded? _____
5. In which regions were two beliefs founded? _____
6. Which belief system has no single founder? _____
7. For which belief system are *Five Classics* the major holy writings? _____
8. Which of the belief systems shown was founded earliest? _____
9. Which system's founder lived most recently? _____
10. Which two belief systems were founded at approximately the same time? _____

Thinking Further: On which of the belief systems are the dates in the table based? How do you know?

_____
_____
_____
_____
_____

NAME _____

KEY FACTS OF EUROPEAN GEOGRAPHY

CHAPTER 5

✽ Below are six categories of information about the land, waters, and natural resources of Europe. Fill in the blanks, referring to a map in your textbook when necessary.

PENINSULAS

A peninsula is a land area almost surrounded by water. The word *peninsula* comes from a Latin term meaning "almost island." Name seven countries in Western Europe that form peninsulas by themselves or with one other country.

1. _____
2. _____ and 3. _____
4. _____
5. _____ and 6. _____
7. _____

ISLANDS

Name three Western European countries that are islands.

1. _____
2. _____
3. _____

EUROPEAN INDUSTRY

Name three ways in which Western Europeans use their natural resources to make a living.

1. _____
2. _____
3. _____

BODIES OF WATER

Name seven large bodies of water of Europe.

1. _____
2. _____
3. _____
4. _____
5. _____
6. _____
7. _____

INTERIOR WATERWAYS

Name the rivers on which the following European cities are located.

1. Bonn, Germany _____
2. Paris, France _____
3. London, Great Britain _____
4. Rome, Italy _____

COMPASS DIRECTION

1. Which island countries lie west of Belgium and the Netherlands?

   _____

2. Switzerland lies _____ of Spain.

3. Denmark lies _____ of Germany.

Thinking Further: Europe is made up of many independent countries, whereas North America is divided into very few. On a separate sheet of paper, describe three or more ways an American tourist might notice the different countries of Europe.

Creating a Pictograph

✻ Using information in the table, complete the pictograph showing the populations of six major European cities.

a. Write the names of the cities on the lines to the left of the graph. The city with the most people—Madrid—has been written on the top line for you. Put the second largest city on the second line, and so forth.

b. Look at the picture above the graph. The whole picture represents 500,000 people. You can use up to one picture per square on the graph. Use only part of a picture to indicate a number of less than 500,000. For example, draw four fifths of a picture to indicate 400,000 people. That was done to indicate 400,000 people in the line for Madrid. Draw only as many pictures or parts of pictures as needed.

City	Population (estimate)
Athens, Greece	750,000
Bonn, Germany	300,000
Madrid, Spain	2,900,000
Paris, France	2,200,000
Rome, Italy	2,800,000
Stockholm, Sweden	680,000

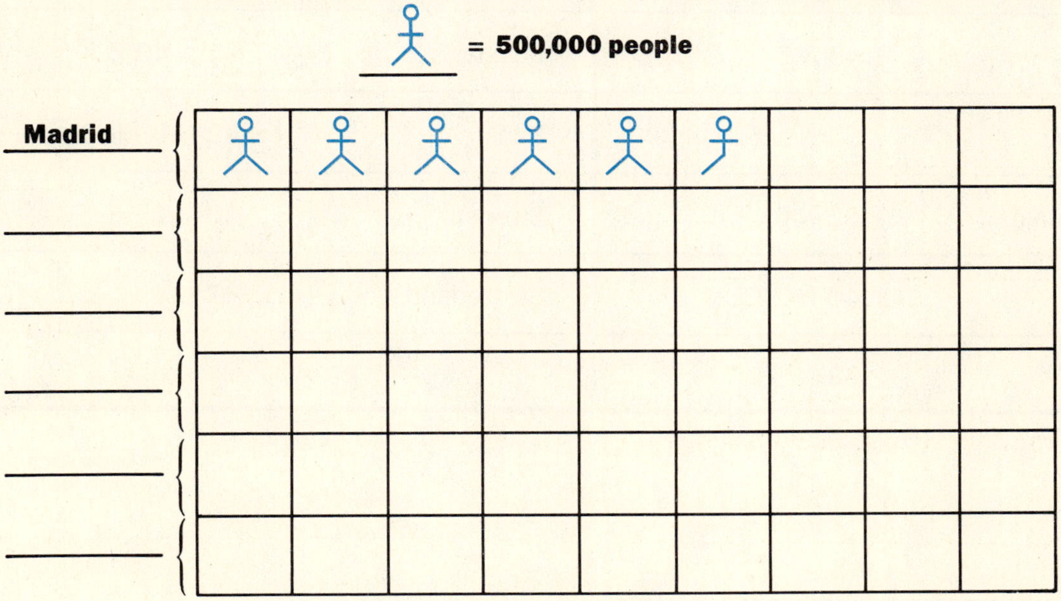

👤 = 500,000 people

Thinking Further: The same information is presented in two forms on this page. Describe one advantage and one disadvantage of each form, as shown on the page.

NAME _____

IDENTIFYING COUNTRIES ON A MAP

CHAPTER 5

✱ The map on the facing page shows outlines of countries in Europe, including part of Russia. The table below lists some of the countries and the latitude and longitude coordinates of a location in each country. For each country, use the coordinates to identify its location on the map. Then write the name of the country on the map. A few have been done for you.

Country	Location In Country	Country	Location In Country
Albania	41°N/20°E	Italy	45°N/10°E
Austria	47°N/15°E	Luxembourg	50°N/8°E
Belgium	51°N/5°E	Netherlands	52°N/5°E
Denmark	57°N/10°E	Norway	60°N/10°E
Finland	62°N/25°E	Portugal	40°N/8°W
France	45°N/5°E	Russia	55°N/40°E
Germany	50°N/10°E	Spain	40°N/5°W
Great Britain	52°N/0°	Sweden	60°N/15°E
Greece	40°N/22°E	Switzerland	47°N/8°E
Ireland	53°N/8°W		

NAME _____

IDENTIFYING COUNTRIES ON A MAP CONTINUED

Thinking Further: Name the countries in Europe that are landlocked and explain why being landlocked could be a problem.

_____
_____
_____
_____

NAME _____

CHAPTER
5

RECOGNIZING THE SHAPES OF COUNTRIES

✱ All countries have different shapes, as well as different sizes and geographic features. Knowing a country's shape helps you recognize it quickly on a map. Below are separate outline maps of 13 Western European countries. They are drawn to scale. Label each country. Refer to a map in your textbook if necessary.

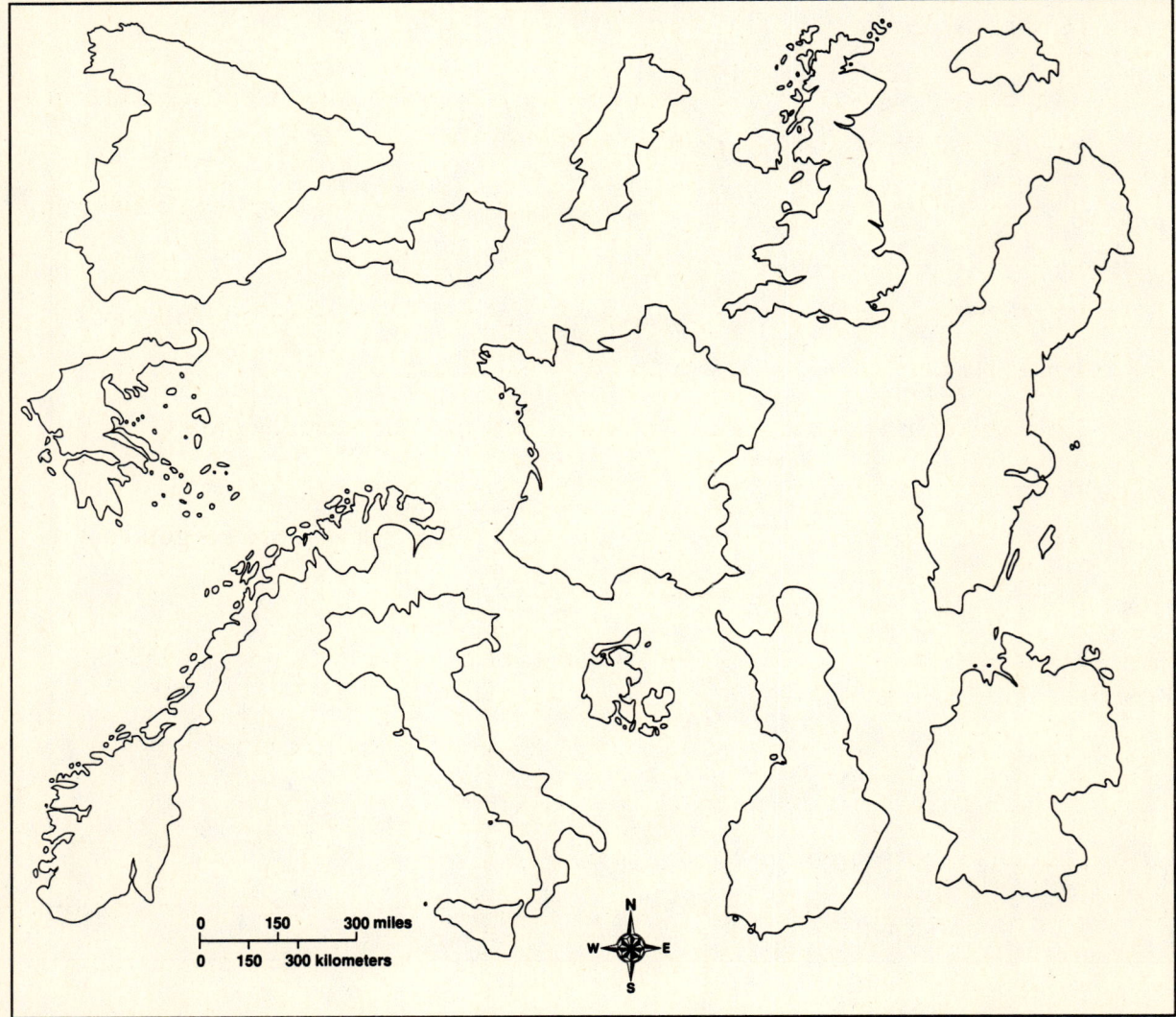

Thinking Further: Referring to the scale and compass above, answer the questions below in complete sentences. Make an educated guess to come up with the second answer.

1. Which is the country with the greatest north-south distance? _____
_____

2. Which is the country with the greatest land area? _____
_____

NAME _____

CHAPTER 6

LIFE IN THE MIDDLE AGES

* To become a tradesman in the Middle Ages, a person went through several steps. The people described below are at various steps in the process of becoming tradesmen. Place the people in the ascending order by writing a number **1** in front of the first step, **2** in front of the second step, and so on. On the line following each description, write the title given to the person at that level of training. You will use the same title more than once. The first one is done for you.

_____ This person has been with an experienced craftsman for three years. He is learning the more difficult skills of a craft. ___Apprentice___

_____ This person belongs to a craft guild. He is teaching several young people his craft. _____

_____ This person receives no pay but gets food and clothing. He does odd jobs and learns the basic skills of a trade. _____

_____ This person has just started a job in which he is paid for each day's work. _____

_____ This person wants to produce a masterpiece, a product that meets his guild's highest standards. _____

* Read each statement below. If it's a fact, write **Fact** on the line. If it's an opinion, write **Opinion** on the line.

_____ 1. Saint Benedict established the Abbey of Monte Cassino.

_____ 2. Life in a monastery was too hard.

_____ 3. Monks spent a lot of time in prayer.

_____ 4. Some of the finest buildings erected in the Middle Ages were cathedrals.

_____ 5. Nuns often did the tasks that teachers and nurses do today.

Thinking Further: Imagine that you are a journeyman silversmith. (A silversmith is a person who uses silver to make fine things, like teapots, candlesticks, and jewelry.) What item would you make as your masterpiece? Write a description of it. Include several details. If you wish, draw a small sketch of the item. Make sure the item chosen can be made of silver and that the details given are relevant to the item.

_____

_____

Chapter 6, pages 179–183

Enjoying Shakespearean Drama

✱ One of the best-known figures of the Renaissance was the English playwright and poet William Shakespeare (1564–1616). Many people consider him to be the greatest writer of all time. Shakespeare wrote many plays that are still popular. These plays include *Romeo and Juliet, Julius Caesar, Hamlet,* and *Macbeth.* The following is a famous passage from Shakespeare's play *As You Like It.* The passage describes seven phases in the life of a man.

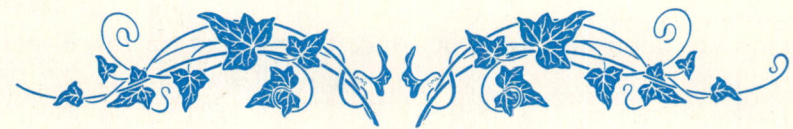

The Seven Ages of Man

All the world's a stage,
And all the men and women merely players;
They have their exits and their
  entrances;
And one man in his time plays many parts,
His acts being seven ages. At first the
  infant,
Mewling [crying] and puking in the
  nurse's arms.
And then the whining school-boy, with his
  satchel [school bag],
And shining morning face, creeping like
  snail
Unwillingly to school. And then the
  lover,
Sighing like furnace, with a woful ballad
Made to his mistress' [girlfriend's]
  eyebrow. Then a soldier,
Full of strange oaths, and bearded like
  the pard [leopard],
Jealous in honor, sudden and quick in
  quarrel,
Seeking the bubble reputation
Even in the cannon's mouth. And then the
  justice,
In fair round belly with good capon
  [chicken] lined,
With eyes severe and beard of formal cut,
Full of wise saws [sayings] and modern
  instances [examples];
And so he plays his part. The sixth age
  shifts
Into the lean and slippered pantaloon
  [old man],
With spectacles on nose and pouch on
  side,
His youthful hose [stockings] well saved,
  a world too wide
For his shrunk shank [leg]; and his big
  manly voice,
Turning again toward childish treble,
  pipes
And whistles in his sound. Last scene of
  all,
That ends this strange eventful history,
Is second childishness, and mere
  oblivion,
Sans [without] teeth, sans eyes, sans
  taste, sans everything.

NAME _____

ENJOYING SHAKESPEAREAN DRAMA CONTINUED

✻ List each of the seven phases in a man's life, as described by Shakespeare. Give two or three details of each phase. The first one has been done for you.

1. infant
   details
   cries, spits up in nurse's arms

2. _____
   details

3. _____
   details

WILLIAM SHAKESPEARE

4. _____
   details

5. _____
   details

6. _____
   details

7. _____
   details

Thinking Further: Do you think Shakespeare's description of a man's lifetime is basically correct? Give two or three reasons to support your answer.

Chapter 6, pages 184–190

NAME _____

CHAPTER 6

EARLY EXPLORERS AND CARTOGRAPHERS

✱ The charts below list important facts about early explorers and cartographers of the Western Hemisphere. Use the charts to determine whether the following statements are true or false. Write **True** in the blank before each statement that is true. Write **False** in the blank before each statement that is false.

Explorers				
Year	Explorer	Nationality	Sailing paid by	Area of Exploration
1492	Christopher Columbus	Italian	Spain	San Salvador; Hispaniola
1497	John Cabot	Italian	England	Newfoundland
1499	Amerigo Vespucci	Italian	Spain	West Indies; Amazon River
1500	Pedro Álvares Cabral	Portuguese	Portugal	Brazil
1501	Rodrigo de Bastidas	Spanish	Spain	Central America
1524	Giovanni da Verrazano	Italian	France	New York Harbor
1534	Jacques Cartier	French	France	Gulf of St. Lawrence

Cartographers			
Year	Cartographer	Nationality	Achievement
1507	Martin Waldseemüller	German	gave the name America to the New World
1538	Gerardus Mercator	Flemish	showed North America with more accuracy than Waldseemüller had

_____ 1. The maps of Gerardus Mercator could have included all the explorations shown on this chart.

_____ 2. The expedition to Newfoundland led almost immediately to the exploration of the Gulf of St. Lawrence.

_____ 3. John Cabot was one of the early English explorers who sailed under his own country's flag.

_____ 4. Martin Waldseemüller could not have included an accurate drawing of New York Harbor on his map of the New World.

_____ 5. Amerigo Vespucci gave his own name to South America but not to North America.

_____ 6. Neither cartographer was of the same nationality as any of the explorers.

_____ 7. Christopher Columbus set sail on his voyages of exploration about seven years earlier than Amerigo Vespucci did.

Thinking Further: How do you think the achievements of the explorers affected educated Europeans of the time? Be specific. Write on a separate sheet.

NAME _____

CHAPTER 6

LUTHER AND CHARLES V

✱ The Protestant Reformation began in 1517, when Martin Luther, a German monk, wrote 95 statements protesting what he saw as abuses in the Catholic Church. Holy Roman Emperor Charles V and other leaders called for Luther to take back his criticisms of the Church. After Luther replied to these leaders, Charles made a statement about Luther. Read Luther's reply and Charles's statement. Then answer the questions.

Luther's Reply

Since Your Imperial Majesty and Your Highnesses insist upon a simple reply, I shall give you one—brief and simple but deprived neither of teeth nor horns. Unless I am convicted of error by the testimony of the Bible (for I place no faith in the mere authority of the Pope, or of councils, which have often been wrong, recognizing, as I do, no other guide but the Bible), I cannot and will not retract [take back] my statements, for we must never act against our conscience.

Statement by Charles V

A single monk, led astray by private judgment, has set himself against the faith upheld by all Christians for more than a thousand years. He believes that all Christians up to now have been wrong. I am now sorry that I have so long delayed moving against him and his false doctrines. I have made up my mind never again to listen to him. He is forbidden to preach and to win over men with his evil beliefs and incite them to rebellion.

1. Does Luther agree to take back his criticisms? _____
2. What would cause Luther to change his views? _____
3. Why does Luther have no confidence in decisions made by the Pope or councils of church leaders? _____
4. How does Charles describe Luther's beliefs? _____
5. What does Charles do to move against Luther? _____
6. Do you think either Luther or Charles V is likely to change his views? _____

Thinking Further: Why do you think people often hold so strongly to their opinions about religion?
_____
_____
_____

NAME _____

REVIEWING EVENTS IN EUROPE

CHAPTER 6

✽ Read the following statements about Western Europe. Circle the correct word or words in parentheses to complete each statement.

1. (Windsor Castle/Runnymede) was the site of the signing of the Magna Carta.
2. Taxes are monies paid (to/by) a king or emperor to help run the government.
3. Magna Carta is (Latin/French) for Great Charter.
4. The Middle Ages was the period in history between about (A.D. 500 and 1500/100 B.C. and A.D. 500).
5. A vassal was a person who owned a (fief/kind of ship).
6. (Feudalism/Monarchy) is the name given to the form of government that developed in Western Europe in the Middle Ages.
7. Castles were built with thick stone walls so that they would be (cool in the summer/safe from attack).
8. Serfs were expected to give gifts to the (king of the country/lord of their manor) several times a year.
9. (Richard the Lionhearted/Pope Urban II) was the person responsible for starting the Crusades.
10. John Calvin led the reform movement in (Germany/Switzerland).

✽ On the line to the left of each description, write the term that is described.

_____ 1. a place where religious men live, work, and pray
_____ 2. during the Middle Ages, an association of people in the same business
_____ 3. a person who worked for another at no pay to learn a skill or trade
_____ 4. Renaissance artist who was also an engineer
_____ 5. a process made easier and faster by Johann Gutenberg
_____ 6. city where Christopher Columbus was born
_____ 7. root word of the term Protestant
_____ 8. the language into which Martin Luther translated the Bible
_____ 9. Queen of England in the late sixteenth century

Thinking Further: What do you think was the most important event (or closely related series of events) in Europe between about 1200 and 1600? Support your answer with specific reasons.

_____
_____

NAME _____

A Revolution in Science

CHAPTER 7

✳ Study the events in the box. Decide which came first, second, third, fourth, and fifth. Then write the events in order on the lines below the box.

> - Galileo uses a telescope to discover four of Jupiter's moons.
> - *On the Revolutions of the Heavenly Bodies* is printed.
> - Ptolemy says the sun, moon, and planets revolve around the earth.
> - Leeuwenhoek's microscope enables people to study microorganisms.
> - Copernicus is convinced the earth and planets revolve around the sun.

1. _____
2. _____
3. _____
4. _____
5. _____

✳ Copy the group of words that correctly completes each of the following sentences.

1. Copernicus did not want to publish his book because he was afraid that _____.

   a. people would scorn him   **b.** he was wrong   **c.** it was not well-written

2. Galileo learned about pendulums and falling objects by _____.

   a. talking with Copernicus   **b.** observing them   **c.** studying Aristotle

3. The invention of the telescope enabled scientists to _____.

   a. study distant objects   **b.** become famous   **c.** work with sea captains

4. Observation and experiments brought about a change in _____.

   a. people's thinking   **b.** the nature of the earth   **c.** lens grinding

Thinking Further: Why do you think people in the 1500s found it so difficult to change their beliefs from Ptolemy's view of the universe to Copernicus's?

_____
_____

Chapter 7, pages 201–205

NAME _____

CHAPTER 7

ANALYZING VIEWS OF OUR SOLAR SYSTEM

✳ The paragraphs below describe three scientists who made important discoveries about our solar system. On the facing page are two illustrations. One shows the place of the earth in the universe according to a theory, or set of ideas, devised in the first century A.D. The second shows a major revision of the theory during the Renaissance. Read the paragraphs and study the illustrations. Then answer the questions.

You have probably studied the solar system in school. Our solar system consists of the sun, the nine major planets and their moons, and a belt of asteroids, or minor planets. All these bodies, including the earth, revolve around the sun.

For many centuries, however, people thought that the sun, other stars, and the planets revolved around the earth. One man who believed this was Ptolemy, an Egyptian astronomer who lived from about A.D. 100 to 165. Ptolemy spent many years trying to figure out how the stars and planets moved around the earth. Scientists later gave his name to this theory. They called it the Ptolemaic Theory.

Around 1512 a Polish astronomer, Nicolaus Copernicus, decided that this ancient view of the universe was wrong. He was the first to observe that the sun is the center of our solar system and that the earth and other planets move around it. This theory is called the Copernican Theory.

About 1609, Johannes Kepler, a German astronomer, made another important discovery. He observed that the planets do not move around the sun in circular orbits. Rather, they move in paths shaped like ellipses or ovals.

The discoveries of the Renaissance scientists Copernicus and Kepler made possible much of what we know today about our solar system.

1. Identify and describe briefly the three astronomers mentioned in the paragraphs.

   a. _____

   b. _____

   c. _____

2. What did Ptolemy think was at the center of the universe? _____

3. Who first observed that the planets revolve around the sun? _____

NAME _____

ANALYZING VIEWS OF OUR SOLAR SYSTEM CONTINUED

1

2

Ptolemaic Theory Ptolemy thought that the earth was the center of the universe and that the sun and the planets circled the earth. Ptolemy also believed the planets moved in smaller circles, called epicycles.

Copernican Theory Copernicus was the first astronomer to observe that the earth, moon, and planets orbit the sun.

4. What did Kepler add to the Copernican Theory? _____
_____

5. What is the main difference in how the earth is shown between illustrations 1 and 2 above? _____
_____

6. Describe two ways in which illustrations 1 and 2 are alike. _____
_____

Thinking Further: For centuries people have observed the solar system and stars. How did improvements in the telescope by Galileo (1564–1642) and others make observing the universe easier?

_____
_____
_____
_____

Chapter 7, pages 201–205

CHAPTER 7

WORKING AS A CHILD

✳ Imagine that you are a young worker in a cotton factory in Manchester, England, in the early nineteenth century. Complete the paragraphs below to tell about your work. Use the words in parentheses under each answer line to guide your writing. For many blanks there is more than one correct answer, so don't worry if a classmate writes in different information.

"What a long and weary day I have! I must be in my place at the factory at _____ (time of day), because that is the time when the _____ (kind of machine) starts running. Then I must work until _____ (time of day) at night.

"The machines in this mill spin and weave _____ (kind of cloth). Before the machines were invented, people did this work by _____ (method). It took _____ (length of time) to learn to be a skillful weaver. But a boy or girl only _____ (age) years old can quickly learn how to tend a machine. And the factory owners do not have to pay children as much as they pay _____ (other workers)."

Thinking Further: In England today—and in many other countries as well—there are laws that say children cannot work in factories. In some other countries, it is legal for employers to hire children as factory workers. The table below lists reasons supporting each idea.

Why Children *Should Not* Work in Factories	Why Children *Should* Work in Factories
1. The work is too dangerous for them. 2. Children need time for school. 3. Children need time for play.	1. Many families need the extra income. 2. Employers should be able to hire anyone. 3. Children learn skills.

Think about the information presented in the table. Then, in two or three sentences, tell whether children should or should not be allowed to work in factories. Support your answer with at least two reasons. The reasons need not be from the table.

_____

_____

IDENTIFYING FAMOUS PEOPLE

CHAPTER 7

✸ Study the information and clues in each paragraph. Then decide who the famous speaker is and write his or her name on the line at the start of the paragraph.

1. _____: "Almost 400 years before I became king of England, King John had agreed to the Magna Carta, which allowed nobles to control the monarch in some ways. However, I continued to believe that a monarch's powers came from God. My son Charles I and my grandsons, Charles II and James II, believed the same thing!"

2. _____: "I was a leader in a civil war to overcome the tyranny of Charles I. Then I ruled England as a dictator. After my death, the English Parliament set up a monarchy again."

3. _____: "I believed that the king had the power to set aside any law passed by Parliament. When my advisors and soldiers began to desert me, I fled England, taking with me the Great Seal of the Kingdom. That way, I thought, no one could issue orders in my place."

4. _____: "My father, the king of England, was so high-handed in his use of power that even I turned against him! My husband William and I later ruled England together. Because we accepted Parliament's Bill of Rights without fighting about it, we were part of a bloodless revolution."

5. _____: "My husband and I were young when we assumed the throne of France. It was such a burden to think about France's problems! We were more interested in wearing fine clothes and attending parties."

6. _____: "During France's revolution, I became so famous as a soldier that I eventually became emperor. I met my downfall when my armies suffered terrible losses during the harsh Russian winter. After that, my weakened troops could not fight off France's other enemies."

Thinking Further: Which of the above people do you think is the most important? In two or three sentences identify the person and tell why he or she is important. Support your answer with two reasons.

_____
_____
_____
_____

NAME _____

CHAPTER 7

RECALLING KEY INFORMATION

✱ First, read the clues and write the appropriate word in the blanks. (A few blanks have been filled in for you.) Then write the circled letters in the blanks in the box below.

1. A person who wants to make extreme, or very great, changes in a short time:
   r a d _ (_) _ _

2. Science dealing with the study of the stars, planets, and other bodies in space:
   a s t _ _ _ (_) _ _

3. General, later emperor, of France:
   _ _ _ _ _ e o n   _ _ _ _ (_) _ _ _ _

4. Italian mathematician and astronomer:
   _ _ l i _ (_) _

5. Careful study of something:
   _ _ _ (_) _ _ t i o n

6. A turning around or a complete change:
   _ _ v _ _ _ _ _ (_)

7. Late seventeenth-century law limiting royal power in England:
   _ _ _ _   _ _   _ (_) _ _ _ _

8. Wealth in the form of goods or money used for making more goods:
   (_) _ _ _ _ _ _

9. Last name of person who developed the microscope to see microorganisms:
   _ _ _ (_) _ _ _ _ _ _

10. Royal prison-fortress in Paris attacked in 1789:
    _ _ (_) _ _ _ _ _

    ┌─────────────────────────────┐
    │ _ _ _ _ _ _ _ _ _ _   │
    │ 1 2 3 4 5 6 7 8 9 10   │
    └─────────────────────────────┘

Thinking Further: Identify the person whose name is spelled out in the box above. Then, in two or three sentences, tell how his ideas amounted to a revolution in science. Write on a separate sheet.

NAME _____

ANALYZING WORLD WAR I

CHAPTER 8

✴ Fill in diagrams **A** and **B** to show the main countries involved in World War I. Choose the names of countries from the countries box. You will use some names more than once. The first name is filled in for you.

Countries			
Austria	Germany	Japan	Turkey
Bosnia	Great Britain	Russia	United States
France	Italy	Serbia	

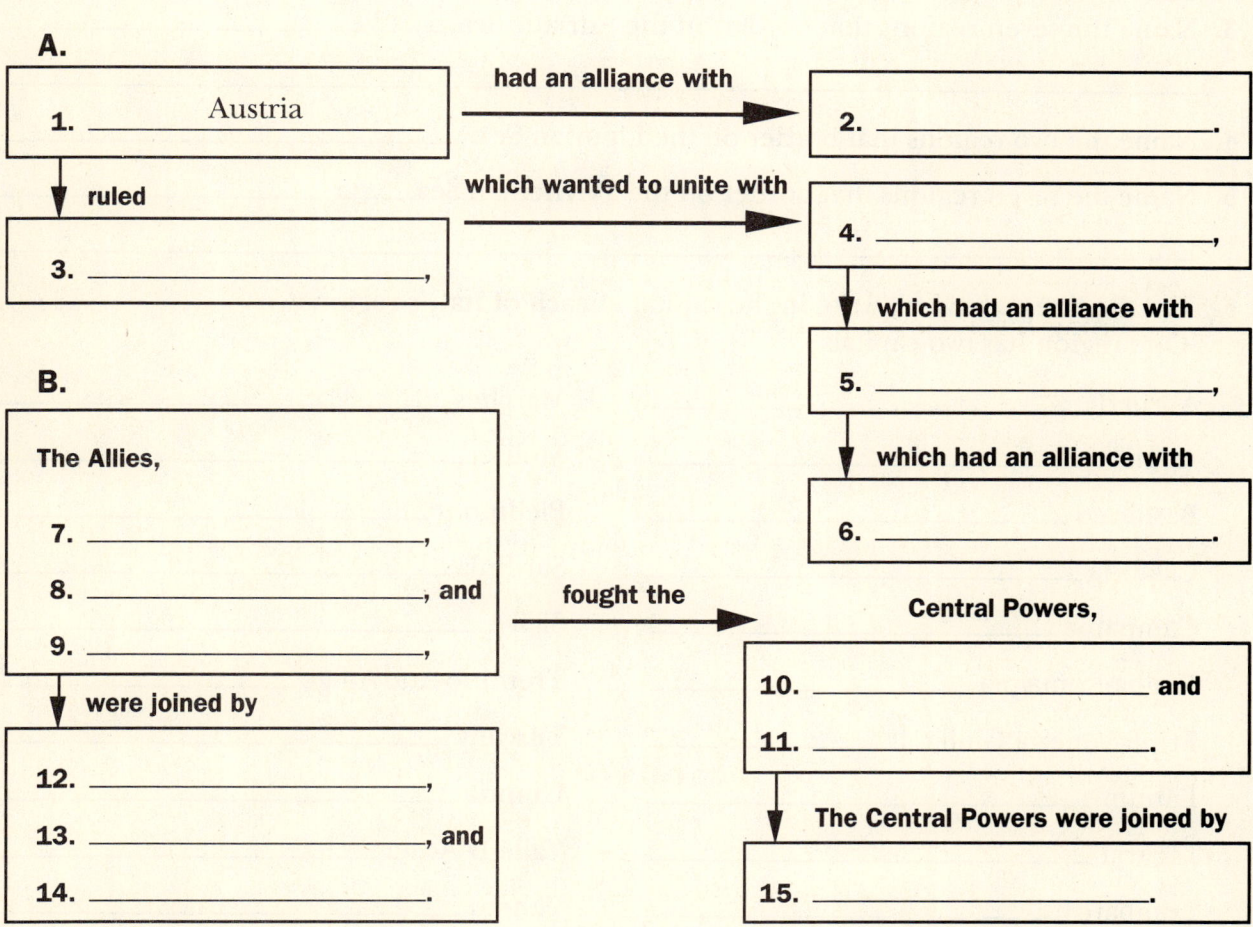

Thinking Further: The war of 1914 to 1918 was fought almost entirely in Europe. Nevertheless, it is called a *world* war. Why is this so?

_____
_____
_____

Chapter 8, pages 227–234

61

CHAPTER 8

THE REGIONS OF ITALY

✳ On the facing page is a map of Italy in the 1990s. The map shows the country's 20 regions, which are political units similar to states in the United States. The capitals of the regions are also shown. Study the map, and then answer the following questions.

1. Name the 13 regions located north of Molise. _____
_____
_____

2. Name the two regions that are made up wholly of islands. _____

3. Name the seven regions that border on the Adriatic Sea. _____
_____

4. Name the two regions that border on the Ligurian Sea. _____

5. Name the seven regions that border on the Tyrrhenian Sea. _____
_____

6. On the lines provided, write in the capital of each of Italy's regions. One region has two capitals.

   Abruzzi _____   Marches _____
   Apulia _____   Molise _____
   Basilicata _____   Piedmont _____
   Calabria _____   Sardinia _____
   Campania _____   Sicily _____
   Emilia-Romagna _____   Trentino-Alto Adige _____
   Friuli-Venezia Giulia _____   Tuscany _____
   Latium _____   Umbria _____
   Liguria _____   Valle D'Aosta _____
   Lombardy _____   Veneto _____

Thinking Further: Identify an important feature of the geography of Italy and tell why it is significant.
_____
_____
_____

NAME _____

The Regions of Italy *continued*

REGIONS OF ITALY
★ Regional capitals
0 50 100 miles
0 50 100 kilometers

NAME _____

CHAPTER 8

UNDERSTANDING WORLD WAR II

* Below is a box with words relating to World War II. In the blank before each statement, write the word or words from the box that the statement describes.

Blitzkrieg	Japan, Germany, Italy	Britain and France	1945
United Nations	September 3, 1939	December 7, 1941	Poland
Austria	genocide	Joseph Stalin	Soviet Union

_____ This country was taken over by Germany in 1938.

_____ This Soviet leader made an agreement with Adolf Hitler to divide Poland.

_____ These nations declared that they would defend Polish independence.

_____ In 1939, the German army invaded this nation.

_____ On this day, the British entered into war with Germany.

_____ This "lightning war" enabled Germany to conquer Denmark, Norway, the Netherlands, Belgium, and France.

_____ The Germans invaded this country in 1941, and were driven from it in 1944.

_____ Through this policy, the Nazis carried out the killing of 6 million Jews.

_____ These nations formed an alliance called the Axis.

_____ On this date, the Japanese attacked American bases in Hawaii and the Philippine Islands.

Thinking Further: What do you find most significant about World War II? Give two or three reasons for your choice.

_____

_____

_____

NAME _____

CHAPTER 9

A Divided Country

* Study the questions under each map. Then write a caption for each map by answering the questions. Write the captions on the fill-in lines provided.

1. According to the map, what were the two parts of Postwar Germany?

2. When was Germany divided in this way?

3. Where was the city of Berlin?

_____
_____
_____
_____

1. What were the two parts of Berlin?

2. Which four countries divided Berlin after World War II?

3. Which of the four countries controlled East Berlin?

_____
_____
_____
_____

Thinking Further: In 1990 East Germany and West Germany were united to form one country. Do you think this was a good idea?
_____
_____
_____

Chapter 9, pages 247–254

Making a Pictograph

CHAPTER 9

✻ The chart below shows the populations of major cities in Scotland, Wales, and Northern Ireland. Complete the pictograph of the populations of these cities.

a. Write the names of the cities in the blanks next to the chart. Put the cities in the order of their populations, with the most populous city at the top.
b. Draw a stick figure of a person in the box in the key.
c. Draw the correct number of stick figures beside each city name to represent its population. Use part of a figure to represent numbers less than 100,000. The first one has been done for you.

Aberdeen, Scotland	190,000
Belfast, Northern Ireland	354,000
Cardiff, Wales	266,000
Edinburgh, Scotland	420,000
Glasgow, Scotland	765,000

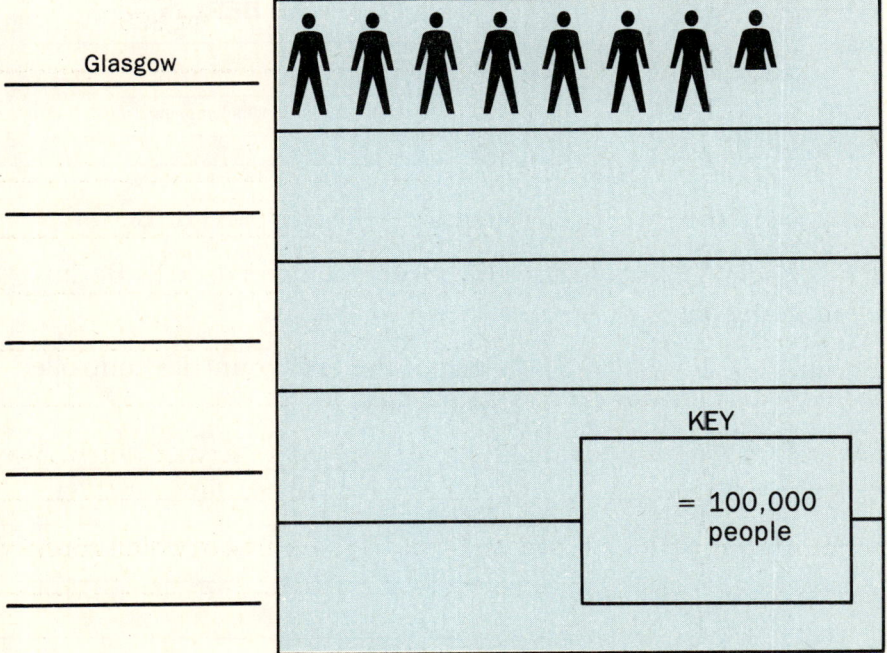

Thinking Further: London, England, has a population of almost 7 million people. About how many times larger is London's population than the total population of the cities on the pictograph? Write your answer on a separate sheet.

COMPARING COUNTRIES AND U.S. STATES

CHAPTER 9

✳ Europe consists of several countries of varying sizes. The largest country in the world, Russia, is partially in Europe. Some European countries are the approximate size of some states in the United States. The following table lists areas of some European countries and of some states in our country. Use the information in the table to answer the questions below.

Selected European Countries	Area (sq. mi.)	Selected U.S. States	Area (sq. mi.)
Austria	32,375	California	158,706
Denmark	16,629	Connecticut	5,018
France	212,918	Florida	58,664
Germany	137,838	Georgia	58,910
Ireland	26,600	Indiana	36,185
Italy	116,313	Maine	33,265
Netherlands	14,140	Massachusetts	8,284
Norway	125,049	New Hampshire	9,279
Portugal	35,383	New York	49,108
Spain	194,881	Ohio	41,330
Switzerland	15,941	Rhode Island	1,212
United Kingdom	94,598	Utah	84,899

1. Which of the countries shown has the largest area? _____
2. Which of the countries shown has the smallest area? _____
3. Which country shown is about the size of Maine? _____
4. Which country is about the size of Georgia and Florida combined? _____
5. Which country is slightly smaller than Indiana? _____
6. The area of Ireland and Switzerland combined is about the same as the area of which state? _____
7. The area of California and Indiana combined is almost the same as the area of which country? _____

Thinking Further: If you knew only the size of a country or U.S. state, could you tell much else about it?

_____
_____
_____

Chapter 9, pages 263–267

NAME _____

CHAPTER 9

Exploring Language

* The English language consists of many words from Western European languages. Use a dictionary to find the meaning of each word in the column on the left. Write the word's meaning in the middle column. In the third column, write the name of the language from which the word came.

Word	Meaning	Language from Which Word Came
1. banshee	_____	_____
2. blouse	_____	_____
3. buffalo	_____	_____
4. cozy	_____	_____
5. dodo	_____	_____
6. gull (bird)	_____	_____
7. mesa	_____	_____
8. penguin	_____	_____
9. picnic	_____	_____
10. ranch	_____	_____
11. slim	_____	_____
12. snorkel	_____	_____

* Look in a dictionary to find a word that comes from Spanish. On the lines below identify the word and tell what it means.

_____

_____

_____

Thinking Further: The English word *spaghetti* is taken from Italian. Does this fact tell you anything about where spaghetti probably was invented?

_____

_____

_____

NAME _____

CHAPTER 10

THE WORK OF GEOLOGISTS

✱ Geology has branched out into many special fields since Alexander von Humboldt visited Russia in 1829. The chart below names and describes some of these fields. Study the chart. Then read the sentences below it. Write the special branch of geology that each sentence tells about.

Field of Geology	Definition
Geophysics	Study of the structure of the earth, and the effect on the earth of weather, tides, earthquakes, and so on
Petrology	Study of the structure and history of rocks
Mineralogy	Study of minerals, such as diamonds
Economic geology	Study of how industry can use coal, iron ore, and other minerals
Environmental geology	Use of ideas and information from geology to study problems caused by use of the environment

1. Some scientists study the structure of the earth in the former Soviet Union. Their field is _____.

2. Humboldt was eager to learn about the minerals in different parts of Russia. He was studying the field of _____.

3. Based on Humboldt's findings, other geologists were able to explore the Urals and find minerals that could be used in Russian industry. These scientists specialized in _____.

4. Some geologists study how waste from industry affects the environment in the former Soviet Union. Their field is _____.

5. Some experts specialize in determining the history of rocks in the Urals. Their field is called _____.

Thinking Further: Imagine that you have been invited to take part in a geology field trip to the former Soviet Union. Choose one of the fields of geology on the chart as your specialty. Write a paragraph describing one or two specific problems or subjects your geology team might study. Be sure to include where your team might go in the former Soviet Union to study the problem.

_____

_____

_____

NAME _____

TRAVELING THE DANUBE

CHAPTER 10

✻ The map shows the course of the Danube River. The river flows through many countries before emptying into the Black Sea. Study the map. Then supply the necessary information below.

1. Area where the Danube begins: _____

2. Western European nations through which the Danube passes: _____

3. Country of Eastern Europe through which the Danube flows just after it leaves Western Europe: _____

4. Hungarian city on the Danube: _____

5. Austrian city through which the Danube flows: _____

6. Site of a wildlife sanctuary: _____

7. The Danube forms a small part of the boundary between Germany and Austria. It also forms parts of the boundaries between _____ and _____, between _____ and _____, between _____ and _____, and between _____ and _____.

Thinking Further: Many composers have written music about rivers and oceans. For instance, the Viennese composer Johann Strauss, Jr. (1825–1899), wrote a favorite waltz called "By the Beautiful Blue Danube." Why do you think composers are inspired by bodies of water?

_____

70 Chapter 10, pages 290–293

NAME _____

CHAPTER 10

REMEMBERING KEY WORDS

✻ Use the definitions to complete the puzzle. Many words in the puzzle refer specifically to the former Soviet Union or Eastern Europe.

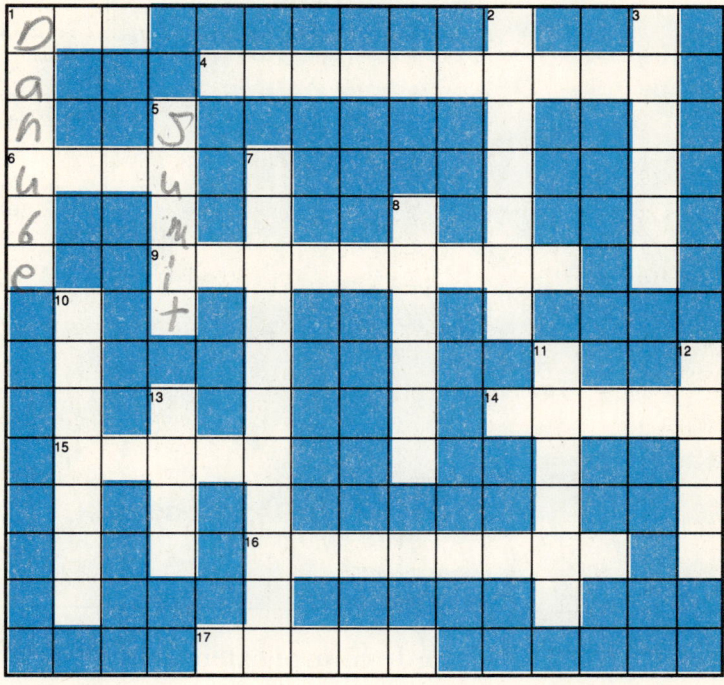

ACROSS

1. River flowing south into Black Sea
4. Layer of permanently frozen earth
6. Abbreviation of the former Union of Soviet Socialist Republics
9. Place where animals (birds) are protected
14. Longest river in Europe
15. Narrow pass between land
16. Another name for a time division (two words)
17. Name of a forest and a sea

DOWN

1. River that flows from the Black Forest to the Black Sea
2. Short saying
3. Treeless plain in the former U.S.S.R.
5. Highest point of a mountain
7. Climate of most of the former U.S.S.R.
8. Treeless arctic plain
10. This country's capital is Budapest
11. This country's capital is Warsaw
12. Northern forests of the former U.S.S.R.
13. Mountains visited by Humboldt

Thinking Further: What do you consider to be the most remarkable feature of the geography of the former Soviet Union? Give one or two reasons for your choice.

_____

_____

_____

NAME _____

CHAPTER 11

THE GOLDEN HORDE

✽ The map below shows the area controlled by the Mongols, or the Golden Horde. Study the map. Then answer the questions that follow.

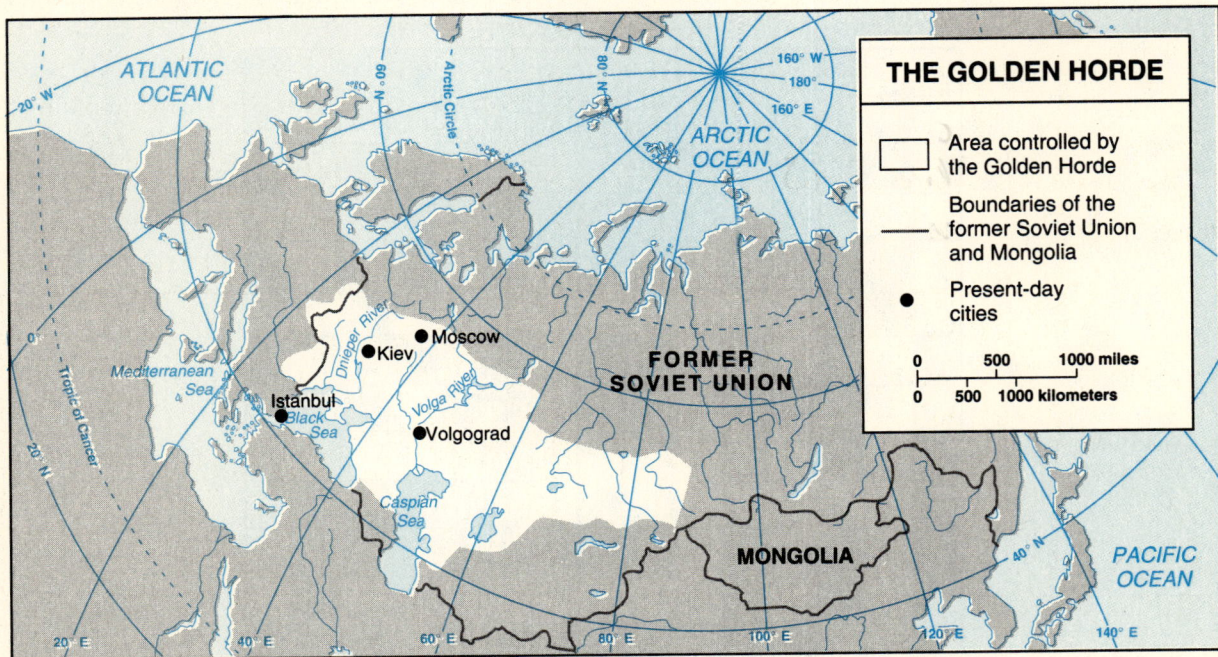

1. Over how many miles did Golden Horde control extend from east to west? _____

2. The capital city of the Golden Horde was near present-day Volgograd. About how many kilometers was their capital from Moscow? _____

3. What river would members of the Golden Horde have crossed on a trip from Moscow to Constantinople (present-day Istanbul)? _____

4. How many miles from the Arctic Circle was the closest boundary of Golden Horde territory? _____

5. By what two ways could a person have crossed Golden Horde territory by water? _____

6. Which river empties into the Caspian Sea? _____

Thinking Further: Why might the Golden Horde not have wanted to control land farther north?

NAME _____

CHAPTER

11

RUSSIAN RULERS

✱ Study the time line of Russian rulers and the table of important events in American and world history below.

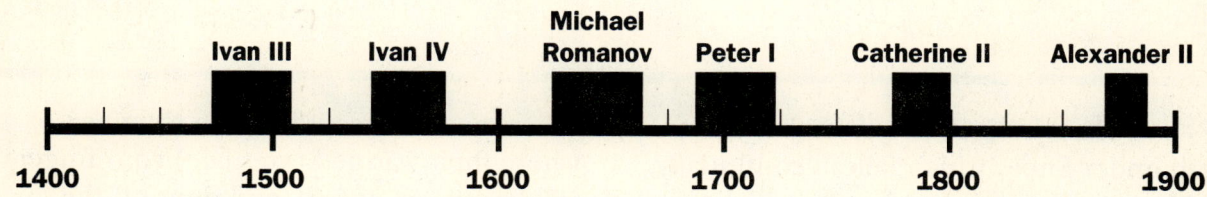

SELECTED MAJOR EVENTS

- The American Revolution—1776–1781
- Sir Francis Drake circumnavigates the earth—1577–1580
- Columbus arrives in America—1492
- The Emancipation Proclamation—1863
- The Pilgrims land at Massachusetts—1620

✱ Decide if each of the following statements is correct or incorrect. If the statement is incorrect, change the name of the ruler to make the statement correct.

1. The Russian czar who was in power when Sir Francis Drake sailed around the world was Ivan III.

2. News of Columbus's arrival in America might have reached Ivan I.

3. Alexander II freed the serfs in Russia in 1861, before Abraham Lincoln issued the Emancipation Proclamation in the United States.

4. The Pilgrims' first Thanksgiving took place during the reign of Peter I.

5. Peter I was probably aware of the American fight for independence.

6. Ivan III and Peter I ruled the same number of years.

7. Ivan III and Catherine II each ruled during two different centuries.

Thinking Further: What are some reasons that news of events in America might not have reached Russia until long after the events occurred?

_____

_____

_____

Chapter 11, pages 308–314

NAME _____

CHAPTER 11

WINTERING IN RUSSIA

* In 1588, a poet named Giles Fletcher traveled to Russia. The passage below, in the spelling of his time, is Fletcher's description of the harsh winter he experienced. Read the passage. Then answer the questions that follow.

... The whole Countrey in the Winter lyeth under Snow, which falleth continually, and is sometimes of a yard or two thicke, but greater towards the North. The Rivers and other waters are all frozen up, a yard or more thicke, how swift or broad soever they bee: and this continueth commonly five monethes ... from the beginning of November, till towards the end of March, what time the Snow beginneth to melt. ... The sharpenesse of the ayre [air] you may judge of by this: for the water dropped downe or cast up into the ayre, congealeth into Ice before it come to the ground. In the extremitie of Winter, if you hold a Pewter dish or pot in your hand, or any other metall (except in some chamber where their warme Stoves bee) your fingers will freeze fast unto it, and draw off the skinne at the parting. ... Divers not onely that travell abroad, but in the very Markets, and streets of their Townes, are mortally pinched and killed withall; so that you shall see many drop downe in the Streets, many Travellers brought into the Townes sitting dead and stiffe in their Sleds. ... Many times (when the winter is very hard and extreame) the Beares and Wolves issue by troupes out of the woods driven by hunger, and enter the Villages, tearing and ravening all they can finde: so that the Inhabitants are faine to flee for safeguard of their lives.

---

1. What does the word *congealeth* in column 1, line 13 mean? _____

2. According to Fletcher, how long does the Russian winter usually last? _____

3. According to the poet, what will happen if a person in an unheated place in winter allows a metal object to touch his or her skin? _____

4. In column 2, line 4, what does *Divers* mean: jumpers, hardly anyone, or various people? _____

5. What does the poet say drives wild animals into the towns in extremely cold winters? _____

6. What does *ravening* in column 2, line 14 mean? _____

Thinking Further: What do you think is the most dangerous part of an extremely cold winter? Write your answer on a separate sheet.

NAME _____

READING ABOUT ALEXANDER KERENSKY

CHAPTER 11

✽ Read the following paragraphs. Then put a check in the box before each word or phrase that correctly completes the statements below. One or more endings may be correct.

Alexander Kerensky (1881–1970) is one of the great might-have-beens of world history. Born in the same town as Lenin, Kerensky became a leader of the provisional government that ruled Russia for about eight months in 1917. Given the chance to help bring democracy to his country, Kerensky saw his dreams collapse and the government turn into a Communist dictatorship when Lenin and his followers seized power in November 1917.

As a young man, Kerensky was a well-known lawyer. He supported a democratic revolution in Russia. Although he favored Russian involvement in World War I, he thought that Czar Nicholas II conducted the war effort badly. Therefore, Kerensky became a leader in the movement to overthrow the czar. After the czar was replaced by a provisional government, Russians looked to Kerensky to solve the country's problems.

Kerensky was popular for a short time. A brilliant speaker, he initiated important reforms. All Russians were given the right to vote. Kerensky also supported equal rights for women and freedom of the press and of worship. Kerensky did not, however, bring peace, and as World War I continued support for him faded. Using the peace issue, the Communists campaigned tirelessly against Kerensky. When the Communists seized power, Kerensky could do no more than flee to Western Europe. He later settled in the United States.

---

1. Kerensky was a prominent
   ☐ Communist.
   ☐ lawyer.
   ☐ revolutionary.

2. Kerensky stayed in office for
   ☐ one year.
   ☐ several months.
   ☐ seven years.

3. Kerensky supported
   ☐ equal rights for women.
   ☐ freedom of the press.
   ☐ the overthrow of the czar.

4. Russian involvement in World War I
   ☐ brought much success.
   ☐ was a major problem for Kerensky.
   ☐ ended in 1916.

5. Kerensky failed to
   ☐ keep Lenin from seizing power.
   ☐ make any worthwhile reforms.
   ☐ stick to his own principles.

6. Kerensky fled to
   ☐ Russia.
   ☐ Argentina.
   ☐ Western Europe.

Thinking Further: On a separate sheet, explain why you think Kerensky was popular with American and Western European leaders.

LEARNING ABOUT SOVIET LEADERS

CHAPTER 12

✻ Generally, the head of the Soviet Communist party was the most powerful leader in the Soviet Union. In the box is a list of the major leaders of the Soviet Union from 1917 to 1991. The list also includes the year each leader became head of the Communist party.

a. Place the letter before each Soviet leader in its proper box on the time line.

b. Referring to the time line, answer the questions below. The time line shows when some Presidents of the United States took office.

> **A.** Nikita Khrushchev, 1953
> **B.** Mikhail Gorbachev, 1985
> **C.** Nikolai Lenin, 1917
> **D.** Leonid Brezhnev, 1964
> **E.** Joseph Stalin, 1922

1. Which Communist Party leader listed had the shortest term? _____
2. Which Soviet leader listed had the longest term? _____
3. Which Soviet leader took office the year Eisenhower became President of the United States? _____
4. How long was Khrushchev's term as party leader? _____
5. How long was Lenin's term? _____
6. Who was President of the United States when Gorbachev took office? _____

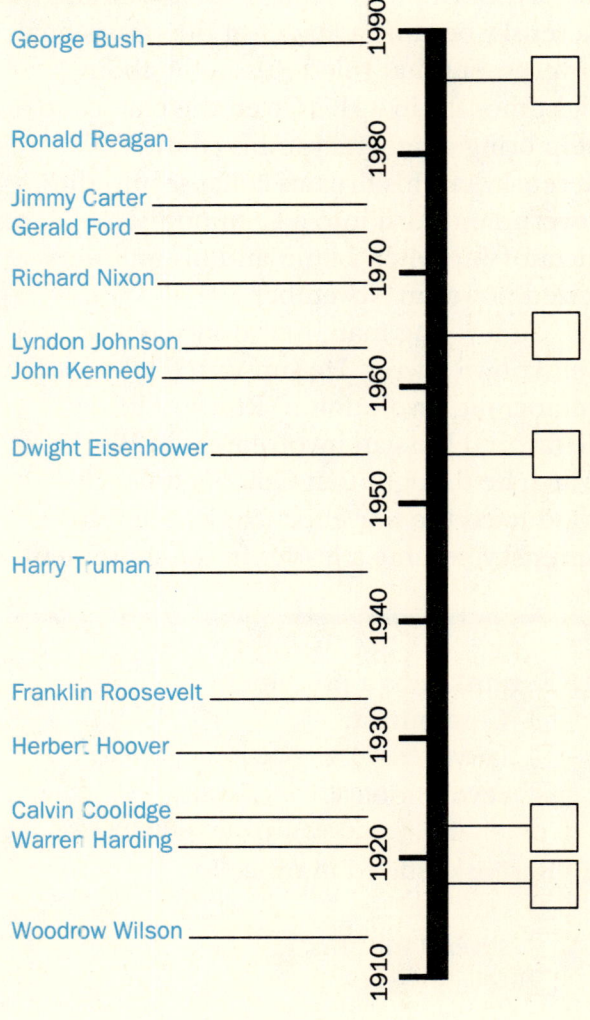

Thinking Further: Do you think it is a good idea for leaders of a country to hold office for more than ten years? Support your answer with specific reasons.

_____
_____
_____

The Changing Soviet Union

CHAPTER 12

* Graphs A and B show the population of the Soviet Union by age in 1983 and 1989. Graphs C and D show the types of jobs held by this country's workers in 1983 and 1989. Refer to the graphs to complete the sentences below by underlining the correct item or items.

1. Graphs (A, B, C, D) tell about the age breakdown of the Soviet Union.

2. Graphs A and B (show, do not show) that the total population of the Soviet Union grew from 1983 to 1989.

3. The percentage of people in the 20–59 age group (increased, decreased, remained about the same) from 1983 to 1989.

4. The percentage of people aged 60+ (increased, decreased, remained about the same) from 1983 to 1989.

5. Graphs (A, B, C, D) tell about the major divisions of the labor force in the Soviet Union.

6. In 1989 the largest percentage of Soviet workers was employed in (agriculture, manufacturing, services).

7. The percentage of people working in agriculture (increased, decreased, remained the same) from 1983 to 1989.

8. The percentage of people working in manufacturing (increased, decreased, remained the same) from 1983 to 1989.

A. Soviet Population by Age, 1983

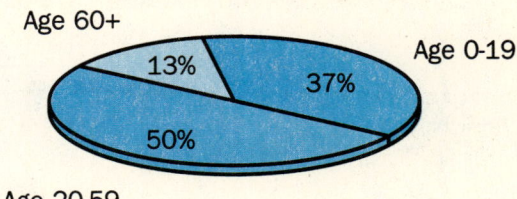

B. Soviet Population by Age, 1989

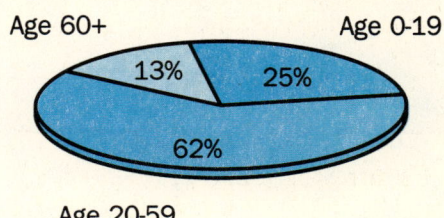

C. Soviet Workers by Occupation, 1983

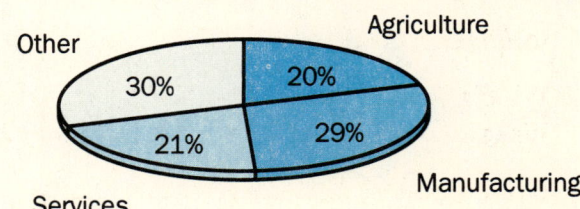

D. Soviet Workers by Occupation, 1989

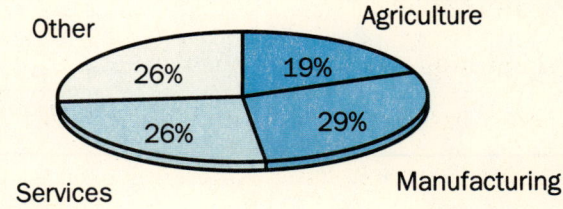

Thinking Further: How do graphs A and B suggest that the population of the Soviet Union as a whole became older between 1983 and 1989?

_____

_____

_____

NAME _____

RECOGNIZING COUNTRIES

CHAPTER *12*

✳ Below are outlines of the countries of Eastern Europe and Russia. The countries are drawn to scale. Write the name of the country on each outline. One has been written in for you. (You may want to look at a map in the textbook.)

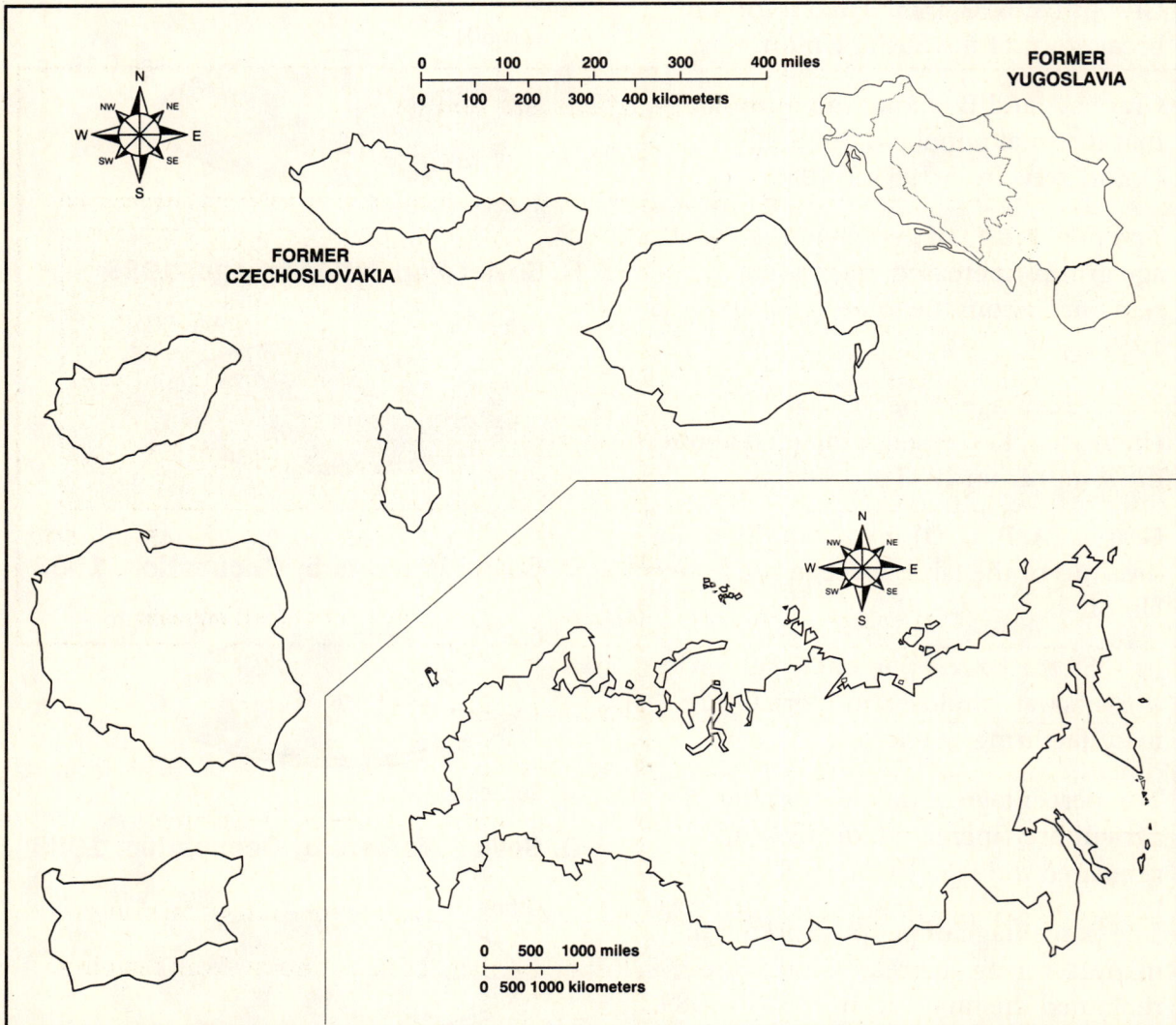

Thinking Further: Describe one or two ways it can be helpful to know the shape and size of a country.

_____

_____

_____

Chapter 12, pages 323–346

NAME _____

CHAPTER

12

FARMING IN SOUTHEASTERN EUROPE

✻ Farming makes up at least 20 percent of the economy of each of the countries of southeastern Europe shown on the bar graph below. Each country raises many farm animals, such as dairy cows, beef cattle, and hogs. Note that the graph has two scales. The scale at the top shows the percentage of the economy from farming. The one at the bottom shows the number of farm animals in millions. Use the graph to complete the statements.

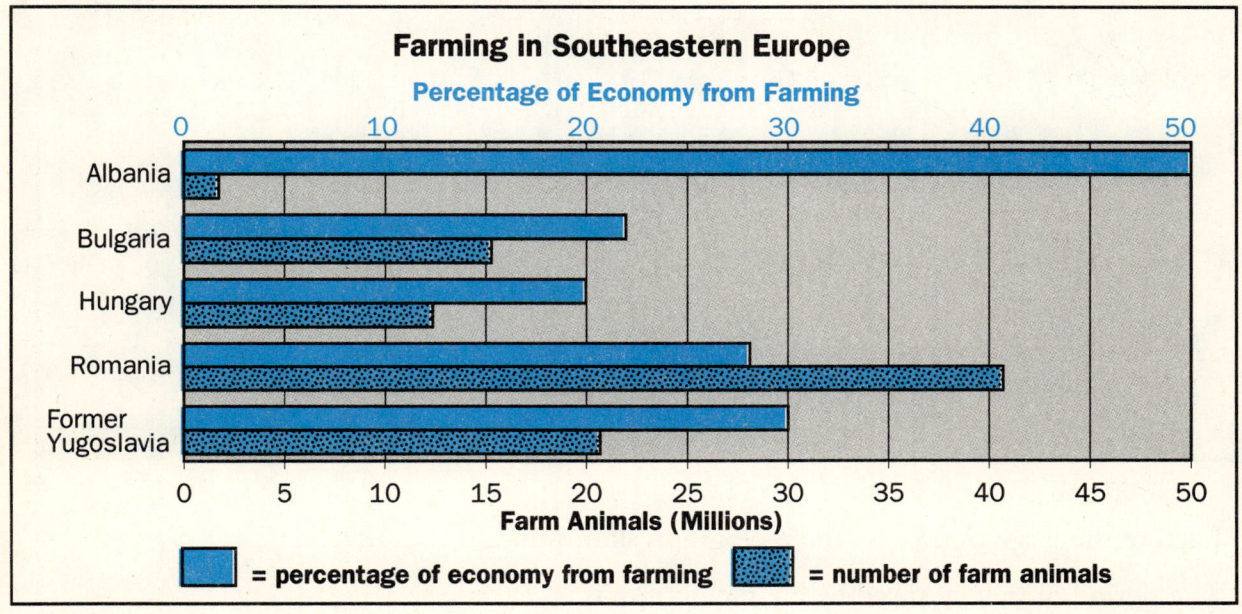

1. _____ raises the most farm animals.

2. _____ raises the fewest farm animals.

3. _____ raises about twice as many farm animals as the former Yugoslavia.

4. About 22 percent of the economy of _____ comes from farming.

5. _____ derives the smallest percentage of its economy from farming.

6. _____ raises just under 2 million farm animals.

7. About 27 percent of _____ economy comes from farming.

Thinking Further: Briefly describe two or three major farm products. What is each used for?

_____

_____

Chapter 12, pages 341–346

NAME _____

CHAPTER 13

POPULATION CHANGES IN THE MIDDLE EAST

✳ Study the pictograph of population in Middle East countries. Then complete the statements.

Population of Middle East countries in 1984 and 1991.

Algeria	1984	👤👤👤👤
	1991	👤👤👤👤👤
Egypt	1984	👤👤👤👤👤👤👤👤👤
	1991	👤👤👤👤👤👤👤👤👤👤👤
Saudi Arabia	1984	👤👤
	1991	👤👤👤
Iran	1984	👤👤👤👤👤👤👤👤
	1991	👤👤👤👤
Libya	1984	╎
	1991	👤

👤 = 5 million people

1. Each of the large figures on the pictograph stands for _____.

2. The period of time covered by the pictograph is _____.

3. The Middle East country shown with the largest population in 1984 was _____

4. The country shown with the smallest population is _____, which had just over _____ in 1991.

5. _____ and _____ had the smallest growth in population of the countries shown from 1984 to 1991.

6. _____ had a population growth of about 15 million in the 7 years shown.

7. _____ had a population increase in the five-year period shown.

Thinking Further: What impact do you think the increase in population has on the economy of a country?

_____

_____

NAME _____

CHAPTER 13

THE VASTNESS OF THE DESERTS

✳ The bar graph below shows how much land in some countries of North Africa and the Middle East is desert. Study the graph, and then answer the questions.

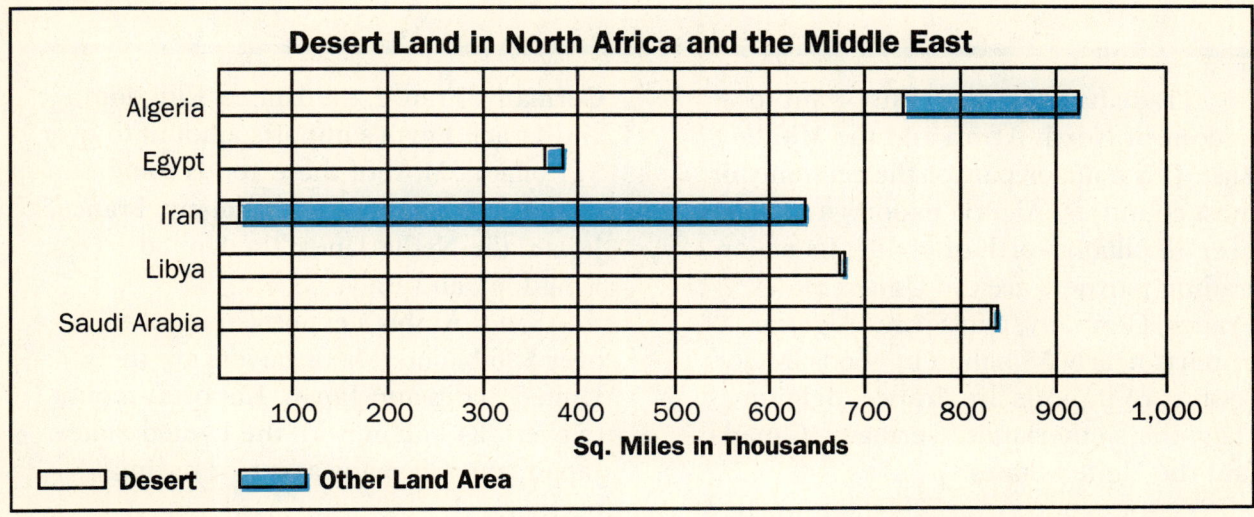

1. Which of the countries shown has the largest total land area? _____
2. Which of the countries shown contains the largest area of desert? _____
3. Which country has the smallest total land area? _____
4. Which country has the smallest desert area? _____
5. Which two countries have the smallest areas of non-desert land? _____

✳ How do the land areas in these countries compare to sizes of American states? Draw a line from each area on the left to the state closest to it in size. One state is used twice.

Desert area of Algeria   Indiana, 36,185 square miles

Total land area of Egypt   California, 158,706 square miles

Total land area of Iran   Alaska, 586,412 square miles

Non-desert land of Algeria   Texas, 266,807 square miles

Desert land of Iran

Thinking Further: What part of a country's economy is most affected if large areas of the country are desert? Give a reason for your answer.

_____
_____
_____

Chapter 13, pages 363–366

NAME _____

CHAPTER

13

TRACING THE PATHS OF TRADE

✱ Read the article below about import and export trade by nations in North Africa and the Middle East. Use the information in the article to complete the table on the facing page.

Trade has long been important to nations of North Africa and the Middle East. It is a major part of the economy of most countries. Algeria exports a total of over $8 billion worth of goods. Its major trading partners are the United States, France, Germany, and Spain. Algeria imports nearly $8 billion in goods. Major sources of imports are France, Belgium, Italy, the Netherlands, Germany, Canada, and the United States.

Egypt exports over $3 billion worth of goods to the United States, Japan, Italy, Germany, France, the United Kingdom, and Israel. Egypt's imports amount to over $11 billion. Most of these goods come from the United States, Germany, France, Japan, the Netherlands, the United Kingdom, and Italy.

Saudi Arabia's exports amount to over $26 billion. Major buyers are the United States and Japan. Imports amount to over $24 billion, with the United States, Japan, and Germany as major trading partners.

✱ Use the information on the table to answer the questions below.

1. Which countries on the table are major trading partners of the United States? _____
_____

2. Which country on the table has no major trade with Japan? _____

3. Which country's imports exceed its exports by $8 billion? _____

4. Which country's exports exceed its imports by about $2 billion? _____

5. Which of the countries that Algeria trades with do not receive many of Algeria's exports?
_____

Thinking Further: Which total, imports or exports, is probably the greatest when a country has a strong economy? Give a reason for your answer.

_____
_____
_____
_____

NAME _____

TRACING THE PATHS OF TRADE CONTINUED

Country	Exports to:	Value of Exports (dollars)	Imports From:	Value of Imports (dollars)
Algeria	United States		France	
Egypt				
Saudi Arabia				

Chapter 13, pages 367–373

NAME _____

CHAPTER 14

CHANGES IN RELIGIOUS MEMBERSHIP

✱ The bar graph shows the change in the membership of four major religions from 1980 to 1994. Study the bar graph, and then circle the correct answer to each question below.

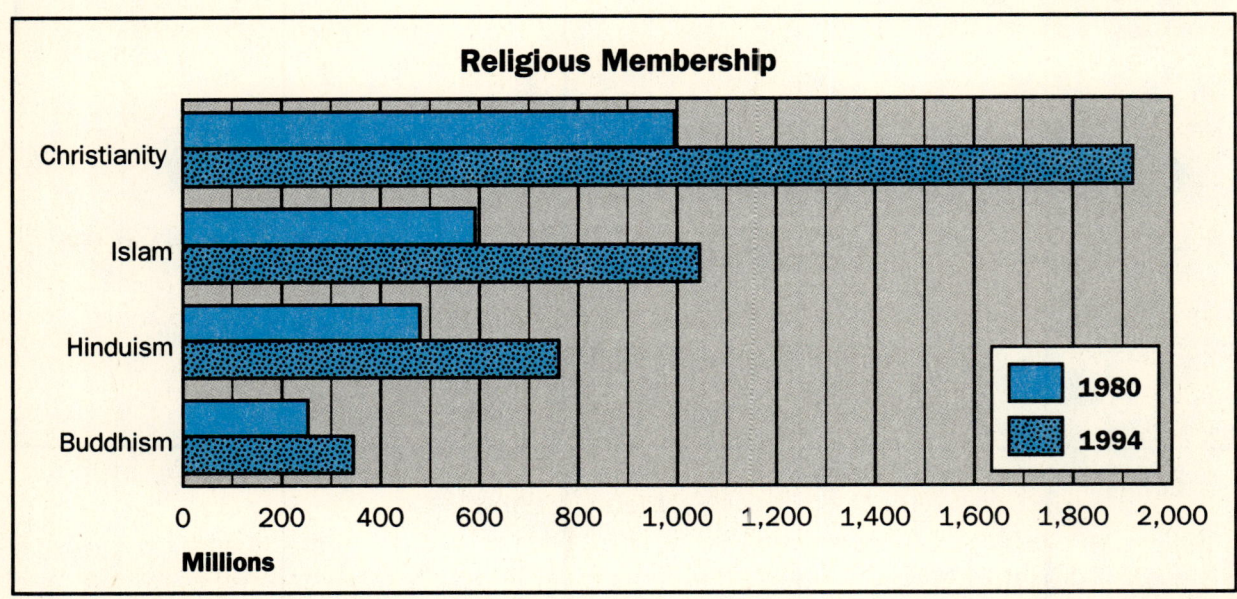

1. How did the number of people in each of the religions change between 1980 and 1994?
   Stayed the same   Decreased   Increased   Doubled

2. Which religion had more than 1.5 billion members in 1994?
   Hinduism   Islam   Christianity   Buddhism

3. Which religious group had a membership of about 300 million in 1994?
   Buddhism   Islam   Hinduism   Christianity

4. Which two groups had memberships under 500 million members in 1980?
   Buddhism and Islam   Buddhism and Hinduism
   Christianity and Buddhism   Hinduism and Christianity

5. Which group grew by about 400 million from 1980 to 1994?
   Islam   Christianity   Hinduism   Buddhism

6. Which group grew the most in the eight-year period shown on the graph?
   Christianity   Islam   Hinduism   Buddhism

Thinking Further: The world population is about 5 billion people. Why does the combined memberships of the four religions not equal 5 billion? Write your answer on a separate sheet.

NAME _____

THE CRUSADES

CHAPTER **14**

* Read about the Crusades below. Then answer the questions.

> **1095–1099: First Crusade**—Crusaders capture Jerusalem and form four states in Holy Land.
> **1147–1148: Second Crusade**—Crusaders, led by the kings of Germany and France, are defeated by Muslims.
> **1189–1192: Third Crusade**—After Saladin and the Muslims recapture Jerusalem, the Third Crusade forms. It fails, but Richard I of England persuades Saladin to let Christian pilgrims enter Jerusalem.
> **1201–1204: Fourth Crusade**—Crusaders become involved in wars in Europe and never reach the Holy Land.
> **1212: Children's Crusade** leaves Europe for the Holy Land, but most of the children are taken to North Africa as slaves.
> **1218–1221: Fifth Crusade**—After seriously threatening the Muslims, the crusaders are forced to retreat because of a flood.
> **1227–1229: Sixth Crusade**—Frederick II, the leader of the crusade, signs a treaty with the Muslims, giving Jerusalem to the crusaders for ten years.
> **1248–1254: Seventh Crusade**—King Louis IX of France leads an attack on the Muslims. The Muslims capture the king and his nobles and hold them until a ransom is paid.
> **1270: Eighth Crusade**—Louis IX leads his second Crusade. He dies at Carthage and his army returns to France.

1. In which Crusade did most of the crusaders become slaves? _____
2. In which Crusade did Richard I of England fight? _____
3. Which king led two Crusades? _____
4. In which Crusade was Jerusalem given up without a battle? _____
5. Which Crusade never reached the Holy Land because of European wars? _____
6. In which Crusade were the leaders captured and held for ransom? _____
7. Which two Crusades were the most successful? Why? _____
_____

Thinking Further: People today support many different causes, such as peace, human rights, or cleaning up the environment. Choose one cause and explain why people support it. Write your answer on a separate sheet.

Chapter 14, pages 386–394

NAME _____

CHAPTER 14

LOCATING IMPORTANT MUSLIM PLACES

✻ The map shows places that are important to Muslims. Study the map, and then answer the questions that follow.

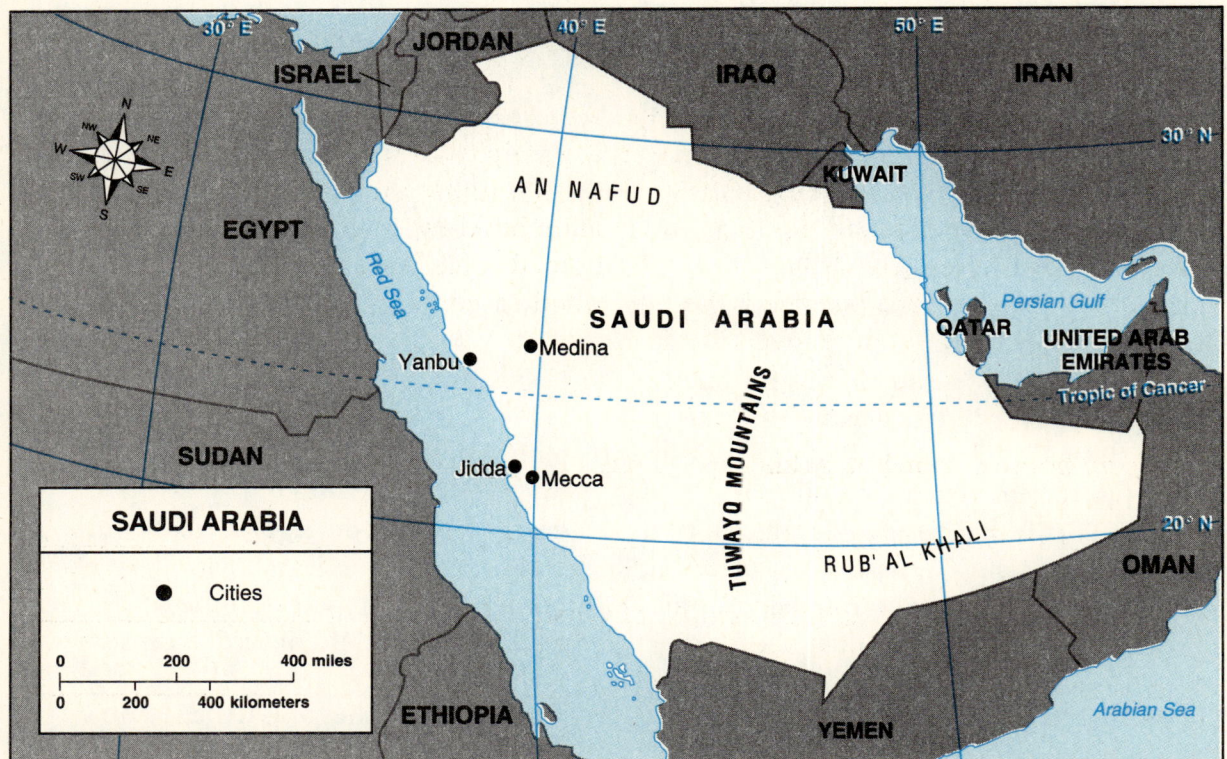

1. In which direction did Muhammad travel on the Hegira from Mecca to Medina? _____

2. When Muslims today retrace the Hegira, how far do they travel? _____

3. What four geographic features may Muslims on pilgrimages to Mecca pass? _____

4. When Muslims in the United Arab Emirates pray facing Mecca, in which direction do they face? _____

5. The Kaaba shrine in Mecca is located in which country? _____

6. How far is the mosque in Medina from the Red Sea? _____

7. Which two cities on the map are northwest of Mecca? _____

Thinking Further: If a map showed your community and other major places within 100 miles, what would it show? Include in your description physical features such as mountains and lakes. Write your answer on a separate sheet.

NAME _____

MUSLIM HOUSES OF WORSHIP

CHAPTER **14**

* Read the following description of Muslim houses of worship. Then complete the statements below.

The Muslim houses of worship, called mosques, are among the most beautiful examples of architecture in the world. Every mosque has a tall, slender tower, or minaret, that can be seen from afar. Another prominent part of a mosque is the mihrab, or gate. The gate is often decorated with intricate designs, and stands out from the plain front wall facing the street. A court is inside the gate and in front of the main building. Many mosques have great domed roofs. A pulpit, or mimbar, made of wood or stone, is the only furniture inside.

1. A Muslim house of worship is called a _____.

2. The gate of a mosque is called a _____.

3. The only furniture inside a Muslim house of worship is a pulpit, or _____.

4. Front walls of Muslim houses of worship are often _____.

5. Gates of Muslim houses of worship are often decorated with _____.

6. From far away, people can see the _____.

7. Some Muslim houses of worship have a large rounded _____.

8. Inside the gate and in front of the main building of a Muslim house of worship is a

_____

Thinking Further: Describe an important building in your community. Describe the building's features and what it is used for.

_____

_____

_____

_____

_____

_____

© Silver, Burdett & Ginn Inc.

NAME _____

CHAPTER 15

IRAN'S PETROLEUM INDUSTRY

✻ The map below shows the location of Iran's petroleum resources and industry. The sale of oil and gas to other countries provides about one half of Iran's total income. Study the map; then complete the sentences.

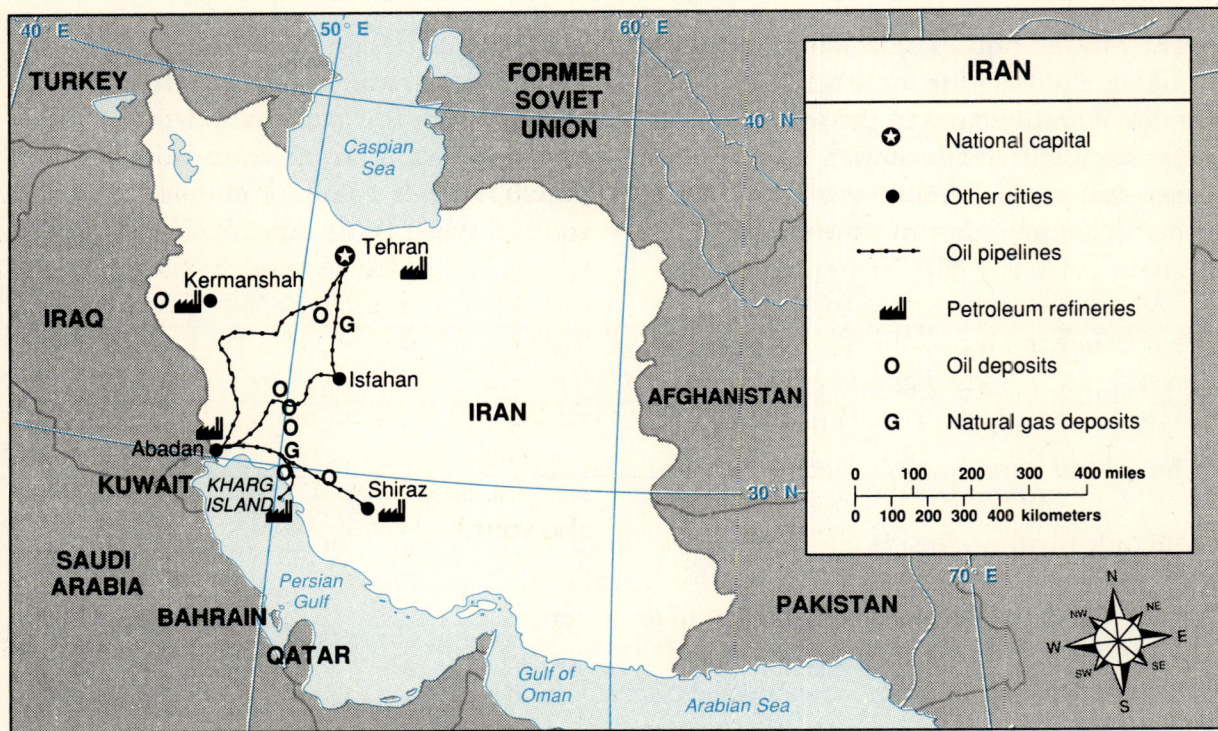

1. Most petroleum and natural gas fields are in the _____ part of Iran.

2. The large island port Iran uses to ship oil and gas is _____.

3. Petroleum from Tehran must travel about _____ miles by pipeline to reach Abadan.

4. Most of Iran's petroleum is shipped out by tankers sailing on the _____.

5. The country closest to Iran's main oil fields is _____.

6. Iran's main refineries are located in _____
_____.

Thinking Further: Write a paragraph explaining how Iran's war with Iraq might have affected the petroleum industry.

_____
_____
_____

88   Chapter 15, pages 403–408

MEETING CHALLENGES OF THE FUTURE

CHAPTER 15

✱ In 1960, Golda Meir, then the foreign minister of Israel, spoke to the United Nations General Assembly. She described problems and challenges facing Israel and other new nations. Read the paragraphs adapted from Meir's speech shown below; then answer the questions.

There are two dangers that face those of us who have emerged as newly independent states; first, staying too long in the past and, secondly, thinking that independence will instantly solve all our problems. . . .

We, the new countries, have gained our independence in an era of man's greatest achievements. In some parts of the world the standard of living has reached fantastic heights. We should not be told to develop slowly; we should not be told that other countries have taken many years or even centuries to develop. We cannot wait. We must develop quickly. . . .

This challenge is one not only for the new nations, but for the entire world. Much has been done to share extra food from the developed countries with people in the new countries who are hungry. But I wish to say that we will never be really free as long as our children need to be fed by others. Our freedom will be complete only when we have learned to bring forth the food we need from our own soil. The cry that goes out from the African and Asian continents today is: Share with us not only food, but also your knowledge of how to produce it. . . ."

1. What two dangers did Meir see for new independent states? _____

2. What rate of development did Meir believe was necessary for new nations? _____

3. How did Meir believe other nations could help the new nations? _____

4. When did Meir think the new nations would be truly free? _____

5. Name two countries Meir may have been thinking about when she spoke of developed countries. _____

6. Where were most of the new nations located? _____

Thinking Further: Why do you think Golda Meir believed people need knowledge as much as they need food? Write your answer on a separate sheet.

ANALYZING A SPEECH

CHAPTER 15

✶ Egyptian president Anwar Sadat's visit to Israel in 1977 was an important event in recent Middle East history. Read the paragraphs from Sadat's speech to Israel's leaders and lawmakers; then answer the questions.

"Any life lost in a war is a human life, be it that of an Arab or an Israeli. A wife who becomes a widow is a human being entitled to a happy family life, whether she be an Arab or an Israeli. Innocent children deprived of the care and compassion of their parents are ours. For the sake of them all, for a smile, for a smile on the face of every child born in our land. For all that, I have taken my decision to come to you. . . .

"You want to live with us in this part of the world. In all sincerity, I tell you that we welcome you among us, with full security and safety. . . . We used to reject you, yes. We refused to meet with you anywhere, yes. It is also true that we used to demand . . . a mediator who would meet separately with each party . . . yes, this happened. Yet today I tell you, and I declare it to the whole world, that we accept to live with you in permanent peace based on justice."

1. Where is "this part of the world" referred to by Sadat? _____
2. For many years, Egypt refused to recognize Israel as a country. For whose sake does Sadat now decide to visit Israel? _____
3. Before Sadat's visit, how did the two nations communicate? _____
4. On what does Sadat want the peace between Egypt and Israel to be based? _____
5. With what does Sadat welcome Israel to live with Egypt in the Middle East? _____

Thinking Further: What do you think can happen to change nations from enemies to friends?
_____
_____
_____

NAME _____

CHAPTER 15

COMPARING OIL RESERVES AND REVENUE

✻ The tables below show petroleum reserves and income for some Middle Eastern countries and the United States. Reserves are oil and natural gas that are still in the ground. Fill in the list beside each chart; then answer the questions.

Country	1988 Income from Petroleum (billions of dollars)
Bahrain	3.0
Kuwait	6.7
Oman	2.2
Qatar	1.9
Saudi Arabia	28.1
United Arab Emirates	3.4
United States	973.6

Top three Middle Eastern countries in income from petroleum:

1. _____
2. _____
3. _____

Country	Petroleum Reserves as of 1988 (billions of barrels)
Bahrain	.1
Kuwait	91.9
Oman	4.0
Qatar	3.2
Saudi Arabia	167.0
United Arab Emirates	32.8
United States	27.0

Top three Middle Eastern countries in petroleum reserves:

1. _____
2. _____
3. _____

1. What can you conclude about the relationship between oil reserves and revenue for the countries listed? _____

2. Where would the United States rank in income and reserves compared to the Middle Eastern countries listed? _____

3. If the United States consumed 6 billion barrels of petroleum each year and used only its own reserves, how many years would its supply last? _____

4. Which of the three Middle Eastern countries listed received the smallest income from petroleum in 1988? _____

5. How much larger are the total reserves of the Middle Eastern countries listed than those of the United States? _____

Thinking Further: Why might a country want to produce its own supply of petroleum? Write your answer on a separate sheet.

NAME _____

IDENTIFYING ECONOMIC SECTORS

CHAPTER **15**

* The pie graphs below show the different sectors of the economies of five North African countries. Study the graphs, then answer the questions.

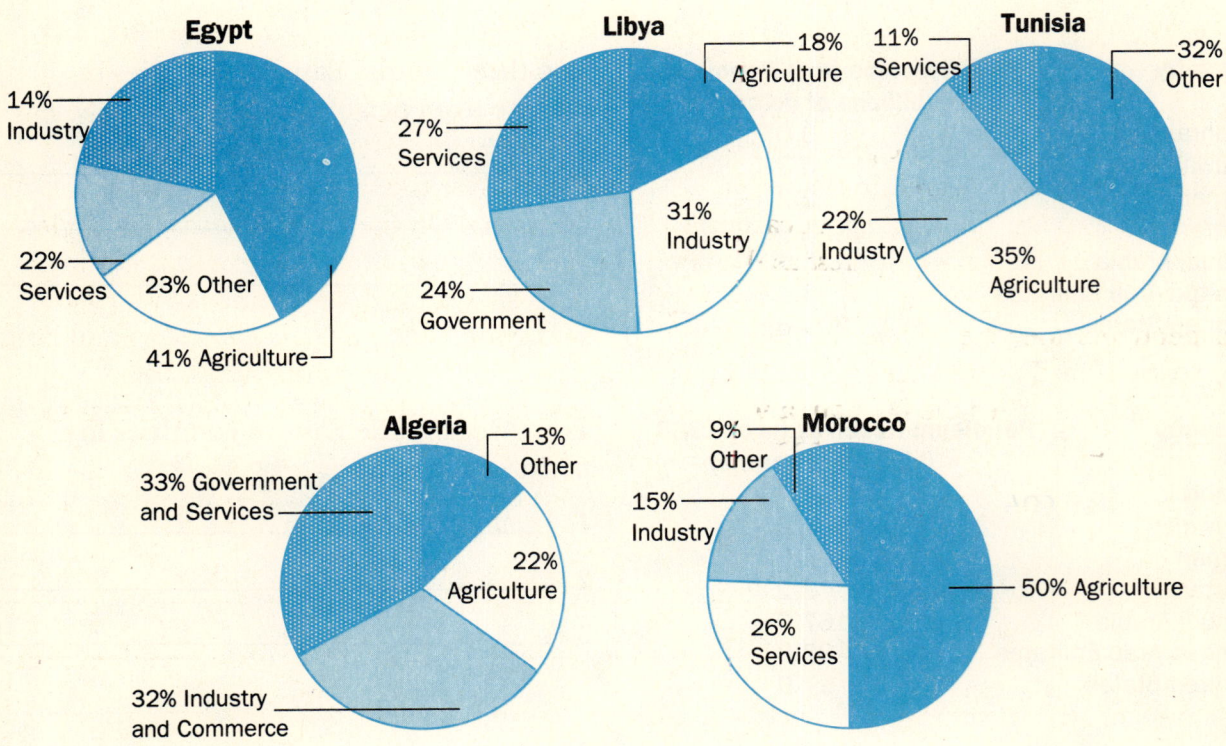

1. Which country shown relies most on agriculture? _____
2. Which country relies least on agriculture? _____
3. Which country has the smallest industrial sector? _____
4. In how many countries is government shown as the smallest sector? _____
5. Which of the countries shown has half of its economy in one sector? _____
6. In which countries is agriculture the largest sector of the economy? _____
_____

Thinking Further: As more people in North Africa move into the cities, how do you think the sectors of the national economies may change?
_____
_____
_____

NAME _____

Exploring Kenya

CHAPTER **16**

* The passage below describes a tour of Kenya. Read the passage carefully, and then answer the questions that follow.

The hot-air balloon glides almost silently over the Kenyan landscape. Slowly it floats over the savanna of the Masai Mara Game Preserve. Below, the grassland and scattered trees are colored in shades of yellow and green. The clicking of cameras breaks the cool morning stillness as the tourists riding in the gondola [cabin] suspended under the balloon capture the sights on film. Two giraffes look up from a group of trees. After the balloon lands, the tourists gather for breakfast. As they eat, they watch herds of grazing gazelles, antelopes, and wildebeests.

The next day, the tourists travel by bus from Nairobi to the town of Naivasha. There they take a boat ride on Lake Naivasha. On the lake, pelicans, sea eagles, and hippopotamuses surround the tourists. Two days later, the group flies by airplane to Samburu Park, where elephants and lions roam freely. The visitors watch the elephants and lions, and feed bananas to the baboons.

---

1. Give five examples of African wildlife mentioned in the passage. *Elephants and lions, feed bananas to baboons, two giraffes look up from the group of trees, herds of grazing gazelles, antelopes and wildebeests, and pelicans, sea eagles, and hippos at the lake.*

2. What four means of transportation are mentioned in the passage? *Hot air balloon, bus, boat, and airplane.*

3. At what time of day does the tour begin? *Morning*

4. Which two communities does the passage mention by name? *Nairobi and Naivasha*

5. What are the balloon passengers doing as they fly into the game preserve? *Filming and taking pictures of animals.*

Thinking Further: People all over the world are concerned about protecting endangered animals from extinction. What do you think should be done to make sure these animals have a place to live and remain safe? *I think their should be stricter laws on animal protection and more game reserves.*

NAME _____

CHAPTER 16

RAINFALL IN ETHIOPIA AND ERITREA

* The average yearly precipitation in a region is a major factor that determines where some people live and what they do for a living. Study the precipitation map of Ethiopia and Eritrea below. Then answer the questions.

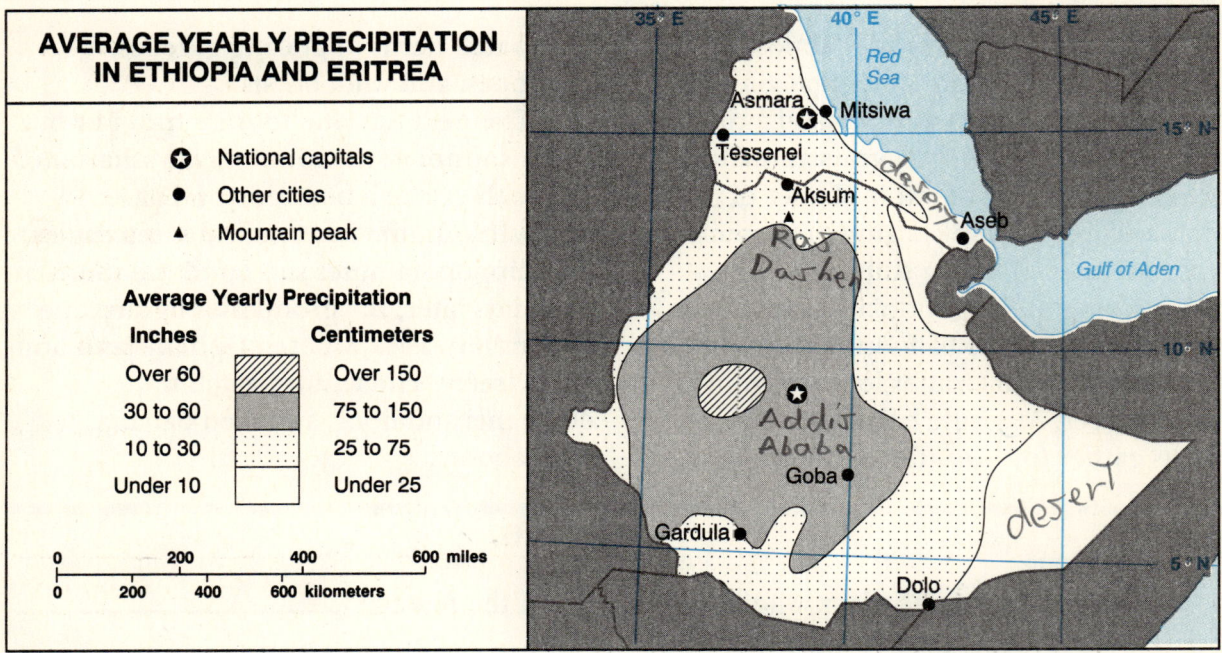

1. The capital of Ethiopia is Addis Ababa. The highest mountain is Ras Dashen. Write these names where they belong on the map.

2. About how much precipitation do the cities of Tessenei and Aksum receive each year? __10 to 30 in. a year__

3. Which region on the map is probably the most populated? __Near the Red Sea__

4. Where would it be easier to farm crops, near Dolo or near Gardular? Give a reason for your answer. __Gardula, because there is more rain.__

5. Where are two desert areas in Ethiopia and Eritrea? Write the word *desert* on those places on the map.

Thinking Further: People live in all areas of Ethiopia and Eritrea. How could they use the land to make a living in the driest regions? __They could make irrigation canals to water the plants.__

NAME _____

LEARNING ABOUT THE FOREST PEOPLE

CHAPTER **16**

* Read the paragraph below about the Mbuti. Then answer the questions that follow.

The Mbuti are a group of people who inhabit an area of Zaire's rain forest. They live in huts made of small branches and leaves. They do not grow food because they do not stay long enough in one place to plant and harvest crops. The Mbuti obtain most of their food by hunting, fishing, and gathering. They hunt birds, antelopes, buffalo, elephants, and monkeys. They either trap the animals in nets or they shoot them with bows and poison-tipped arrows. The Mbuti gather berries, nuts, roots, mushrooms, and honey. When the food supply dwindles, the Mbuti move to another place and set up a new camp. In order to obtain things they cannot find in the forest, the Mbuti trade meat and forest products for goods produced by their neighbors. They trade for weapons, tools, and such foods as rice and corn.

1. Where do the Mbuti live? *Mbuti are a group of people who inhabit an area of the Zaire rain forest.*

2. Where do the Mbuti find materials to build their homes? *They get the materials from small branches and leaves.*

3. Why would the Mbuti have to trade for corn and rice? *They would have to trade because they didn't stay in one place long enough to grow crops.*

4. Why don't the Mbuti live in towns? *Mbuti don't live in towns because the move often and don't stay in one place for very long.*

5. What foods do the Mbuti obtain by gathering? *Mbuti gather berries, nuts, roots, mushrooms, and honey.*

Thinking Further: How do you think road-building and the cutting of the forest could affect the Mbuti and other people who live in the rain forest? *Cutting down the rainforests affects the Mbuti by forcing them to keep moving, and it would scare away game.*

Learning About African Countries

CHAPTER 16

* Examine the bar graph and answer the following questions about the percentage of land that is farmed in each African country.

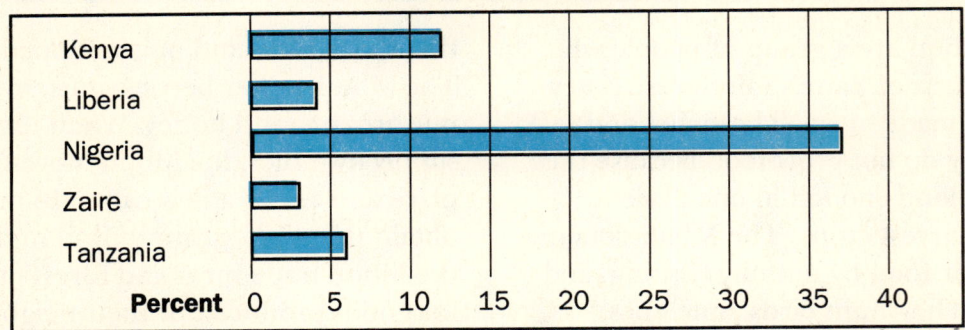

1. Which countries have about the same percentage of land in farms? _Liberia and Zaire_
2. Which country has the smallest percentage of land in farms? _Zaire_
3. Which country has four times as much land in farms as the country with the smallest percent? _Kenya_
4. Which country has the highest percentage of land in farms? _Nigeria_

* Use the following clues to find what percentage of the workers in each country work in agriculture. Write the name of the country in the blank under the pie graph that represents it.

- Nigeria has about 55 percent of its labor force working in agriculture.
- In Zaire, 32 percent of the labor force does *not* work in agriculture.
- More of Tanzania's labor force is in agriculture than any other country's.
- Kenya has the least amount of its labor force working in agriculture.
- In Liberia, about three-fourths of the labor force works in agriculture.

Percent of Labor Force Working in Agriculture

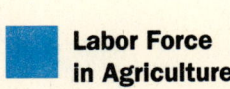 Labor Force in Agriculture

 _Kenya_
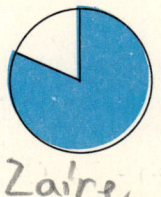 _Zaire_
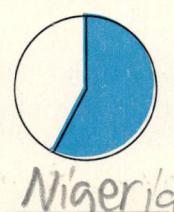 _Nigeria_
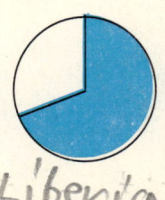 _Liberia_
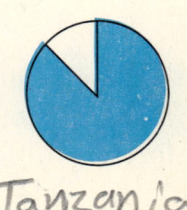 _Tanzania_

Thinking Further: Nigeria has the highest percentage of land in farms. Why do you think it does not have the highest percentage of workers in agriculture? Write your answer on a separate sheet. _I think this because most people are poor and they can't hire people to help farm with them._

NAME _____

THE FEATURES OF AFRICA

CHAPTER 16

✱ Match each term about Africa in Column 1 with its description in Column 2. Write the letter from Column 2 on the line in front of the correct number in Column 1.

Column 1

_____ 1. savanna
_____ 2. Tassili plateau
_____ 3. Kalahari
_____ 4. tropics
_____ 5. Mount Kilimanjaro
_____ 6. Zaire River
_____ 7. Victoria Falls
_____ 8. Great Rift
_____ 9. Lake Victoria
_____ 10. Lake Chad
_____ 11. Senegal
_____ 12. Swahili
_____ 13. Lagos
_____ 14. cacao
_____ 15. wildlife
_____ 16. sisal
_____ 17. Ibos
_____ 18. Sahel
_____ 19. Africa

Column 2

A. region between $23\frac{1}{2}°N$ and $23\frac{1}{2}°S$
B. Africa's highest mountain
C. sometimes shrinks to one third its size
D. "big river," second largest in Africa
E. once fertile, now desert
F. grassland with scattered trees
G. Kenya's national language
H. desert in southern Africa
I. huge crack in earth's surface
J. once ruled by France
K. nearly twice as high as Niagara Falls
L. source of chocolate
M. one of Africa's most valuable natural resources
N. largest lake in Africa
O. fiber plant used to make rope
P. crowded city south of the Sahara
Q. between the Sahara and the grassland
R. second largest continent
S. ethnic group in Nigeria

Thinking Further: People in Africa live in large cities and in small villages. Choose one of these places and write a paragraph describing what living there might be like.

_____

_____

_____

NAME _____

CHAPTER
17

THE KINGDOM OF BENIN

✻ Study the map of trade routes through the sixteenth-century kingdom of Benin. Then answer the questions that follow.

1. Which cities were located in the kingdom of Benin?

   _____

   _____

2. Which cities were situated on the trade route to West Africa?

   _____

   _____

3. Which river would a trader bringing dates and figs to Benin from North Africa cross?

   _____

4. In which direction would a trader taking cotton goods and firearms from Benin to the Gold Coast travel?

   _____

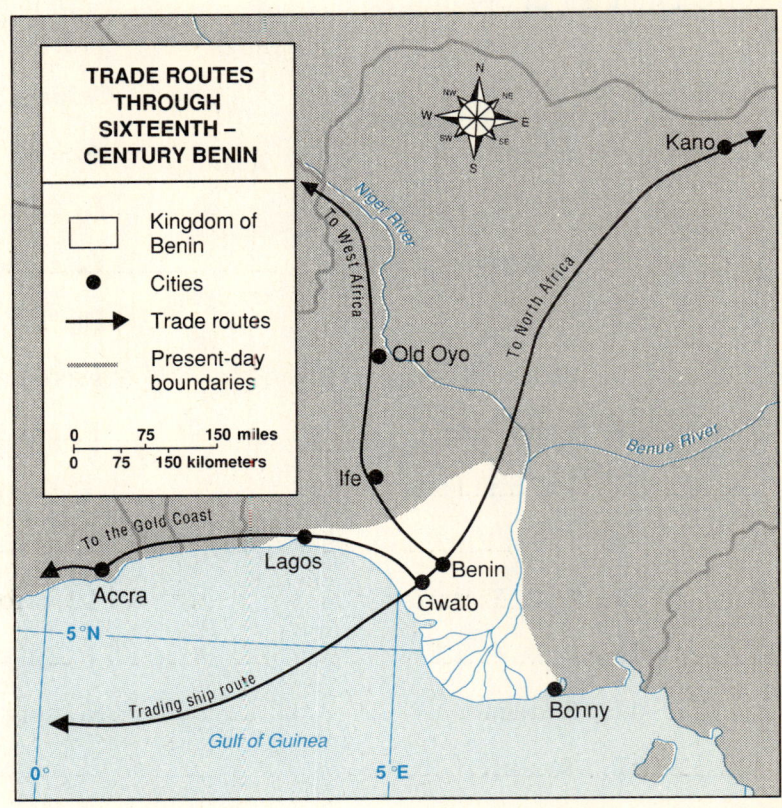

5. How do you think the kingdom of Benin's location helped make it a center for trade?

   _____

6. At its widest point, east to west, about how many miles across was the kingdom of Benin?

   _____

7. About how many miles did the kingdom of Benin extend from north to south?

   _____

8. If a camel caravan from Kano arrived in Gwato, about how many miles had the caravan traveled? _____

Thinking Further: Besides waiting for goods to trade, why else do you think people in the kingdom of Benin might have looked forward to the arrival of camel caravans?

_____

_____

NAME _____

DISCOVERING THE PAST

CHAPTER **17**

✳ The following statements describe discoveries made by archaeologists in Zimbabwe. What might these discoveries tell us about people of long ago? On the lines beneath each statement, write what the clues might reveal about the people who left them.

1. Archaeologists in Zimbabwe have recovered pieces of Chinese porcelain and Iranian cloth. _____
_____
_____

2. Huge stone structures, still standing in Zimbabwe after hundreds of years, were built without mortar. _____
_____
_____

3. Carved stone figures and gold ornaments have been found by archaeologists in Zimbabwe. _____
_____
_____

4. In the Middle Ages, an Ethiopian king had 11 churches carved from solid stone.
_____
_____
_____

Thinking Further: If archaeologists discovered your classroom 1,000 years from now, what would the things they found tell them? Choose two objects in your classroom and describe what they would reveal. (Remember that an object would have to be solid and strong to last for 1,000 years.)
_____
_____
_____
_____
_____

NAME _____

CHAPTER 17

FINDING INFORMATION

✱ Reference books present information in such a way that people can easily find what they need. If you were doing research on Africa, you might look up the article "Africa" in an encyclopedia. The article would probably be organized in sections, such as those in the following list. Read the questions below and decide in which section you would look *first* to find the information to answer the question. Write the letter of the appropriate section in the blank.

- **A.** Geography
- **B.** Climate
- **C.** Population
- **D.** Language
- **E.** Religion
- **F.** Music and Architecture
- **G.** Natural Resources
- **H.** Agriculture
- **I.** Manufacturing
- **J.** Trade
- **K.** History

_____ 1. Which African kingdom remained Christian in the Middle Ages?

_____ 2. What are the main exports and imports of Africa?

_____ 3. What landforms are found in Zimbabwe?

_____ 4. Where is salt found?

_____ 5. How did Swahili develop?

_____ 6. What kinds of machinery are produced in Egypt?

_____ 7. What animals are raised for food in Ghana?

_____ 8. Who was the first ruler of Songhai?

_____ 9. On what waterway was the city of Gao located?

_____ 10. Who defeated the kingdom of Songhai?

_____ 11. What is the major crop in southern Nigeria?

_____ 12. What metals were exported from Kilwa?

_____ 13. What is a monsoon?

_____ 14. What do the buildings of Timbuktu look like?

_____ 15. What led to the downfall of Ghana?

_____ 16. What is the main religion of North Africa?

_____ 17. What musical instruments were originally invented in Africa?

_____ 18. What is the largest city of modern Africa?

Thinking Further: Besides encyclopedias, what other kinds of resources would be helpful for doing research about Africa? Tell what kinds of information might be obtained from each type of resource you name.

_____

_____

_____

NAME _____

CHAPTER 17

THE BENEFITS OF TRADE

✽ Read the passage below about trade. In the statements that follow, circle the phrase that best completes each sentence.

Today, if you needed a new notebook, you would go to a store and buy it with money. You would choose one of the many notebooks the store owner had purchased from a supplier, who had bought it from a manufacturer. The manufacturer produced the notebook using paper from a paper mill, which made the paper out of wood supplied by a lumber company. All these steps from tree to notebook to you involved the process of trade. Trade is the buying and selling of goods or services. At each stage in the process, someone should earn a profit. For example, the store owner may have paid $1.00 for the notebook and sold it to you for $1.50, making a profit of 50 cents.

Hundreds of years ago, traders did much more than supply goods and make profits. Before the development of modern communications systems, the business of trade provided a way for people from different parts of the world to exchange information. Trade routes, both overland and by sea, brought peoples of different cultures into contact with one another. As trade increased, trading centers along the major trade routes grew and prospered. In these centers, people who lived thousands of miles apart learned about each other's customs and ideas.

As time passed, people began to look for safer, faster, and more convenient trade routes. The search for better trade routes led Europeans to find a sea route around Africa and to explore lands previously unknown to them.

---

1. Each step in the process of trade involves (a) a buyer and a seller (b) a manufacturer and a storekeeper (c) a store and a customer.

2. In the process of trade, the goal at each step is that (a) goods are sold (b) the customer is always right (c) someone makes a profit.

3. Trade provided a peaceful means for (a) an exchange of ideas (b) a market (c) a journey.

4. Trading centers grew (a) during times of war (b) as trade increased (c) only if they were on a waterway.

5. People in large trading centers learned more about (a) art and religion (b) other parts of the world (c) remote villages.

6. As some overland trade routes became dangerous or difficult, (a) armies were hired to protect the camel caravans (b) explorers began to search for sea routes to faraway trading centers (c) trade began to decline.

Thinking Further: Besides trade, how else do you think people hundreds of years ago in different parts of the world learned about each other? Write your answer on a separate sheet.

NAME _____

GEOGRAPHY OF NIGERIA

CHAPTER **18**

✻ The following statements tell about the location of important places and physical features of Nigeria. Using the information in the statements, write each underlined name on the map below.

1. The capital of Nigeria is Abuja.
2. Most of Lake Chad is located between 13°N and 15°N and 13°E and 15°E.
3. Onitsha is situated at about 6°N/7°E.
4. Jos is located at 10°N/9°E.
5. In Nigeria, the Niger River flows to the south between about 3°E and 7°E.
6. Makurdi is located on the Benue River.
7. Maiduguri is southwest of Lake Chad at about 12°N/13°E.
8. The city located at approximately 12°N/8°E is Kano.
9. Ibadan is located approximately 2° to the south and about 3° west of the capital.
10. Sokoto is located at 13°N, just east of 5°E.

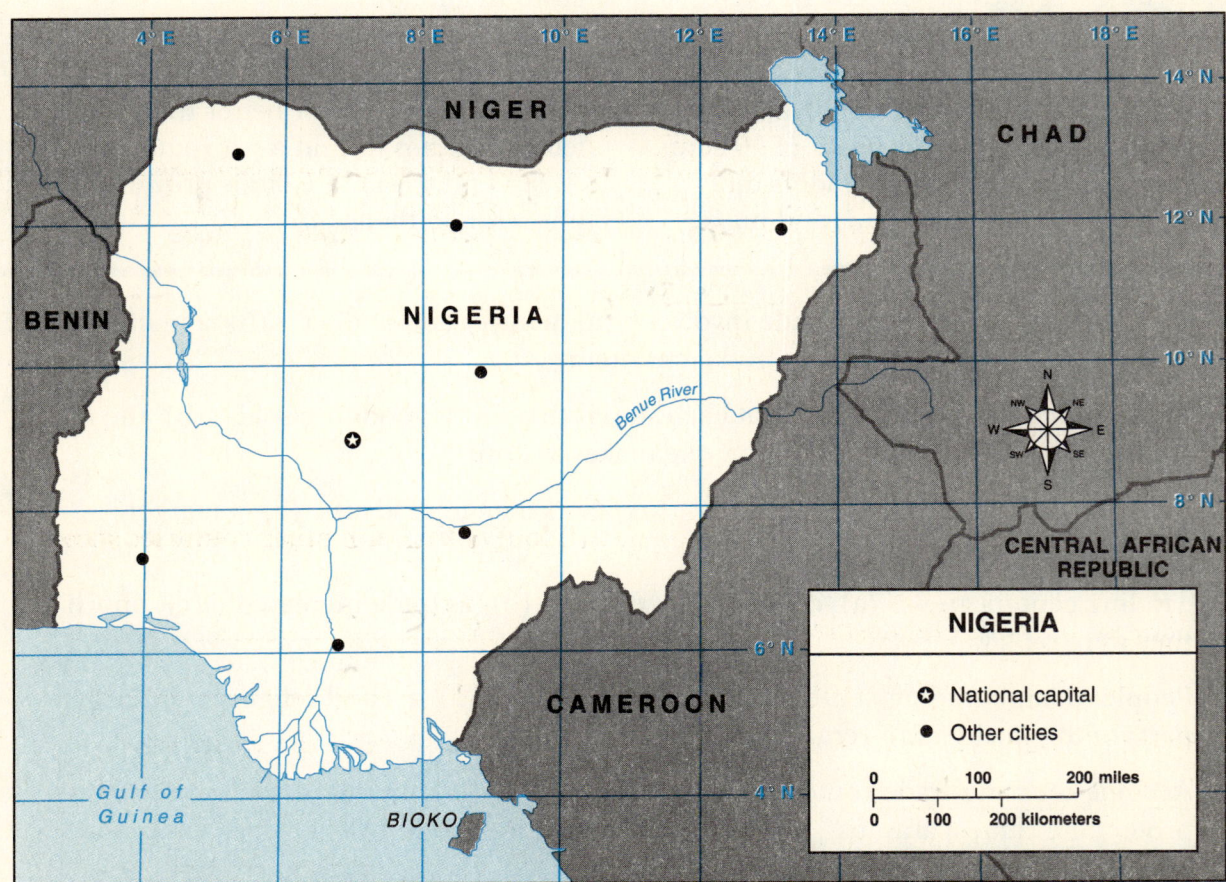

Thinking Further: Identify an important feature of the geography of Nigeria and tell why it is significant. Write your answer on a separate sheet.

NAME _____

CHAPTER 18

INDEPENDENCE IN AFRICA

* Use the information in the list of African countries below to complete the time line. Write the name of each country on the line connected to its independence year. Note that more than one country achieved independence in 1960 and 1964. Refer to the time line to complete the sentences that follow.

African Independence Dates

Botswana 1966	Gambia 1965	Senegal 1960
Cameroon 1960	Ghana 1957	Sudan 1956
Central African Republic 1960	Ivory Coast 1960	Tanzania 1964
Congo 1960	Kenya 1963	Zaire 1960
Eritrea 1993	Mozambique 1975	Zambia 1964
Gabon 1960	Nigeria 1960	Zimbabwe 1980

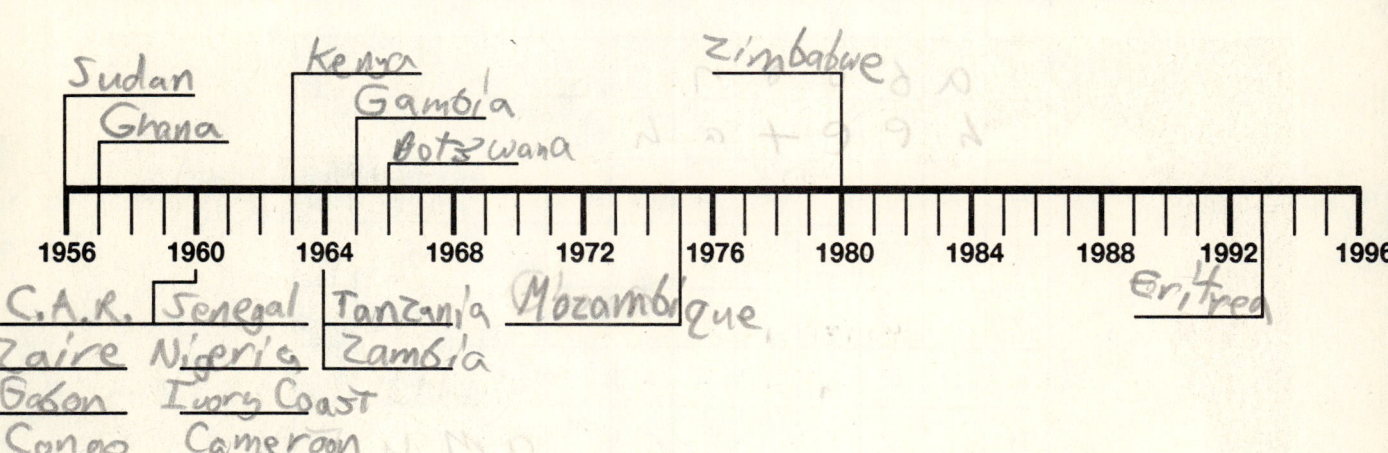

1. _Sudan_ has been independent longer than the other countries shown on the time line.

2. The country with the most recent independence date is _Eritrea_.

3. The majority of countries shown gained independence in _1960_.

4. The only country on the time line that achieved independence in the 1970s was _Mozambique_.

5. The countries that became independent in 1964 are _Tanzania, Zambia_.

Thinking Further: Why do you think many African nations changed their names when they gained independence? (For instance, Northern Rhodesia became Zambia at independence.) Write your answer on a separate sheet.

African Animals

Chapter 18

NAME _____

* Choose the correct African animals from the box to fill in the puzzle below. The first letter of each animal is given. Then, unscramble the circled letters in the puzzle to find the mystery word. This word tells you something about the animals underlined in the box. The first letter is given.

baboon	leopard	giraffe	aardvark	ibis	rhinoceros
flamingo	lion	zebra	crocodile	ostrich	hippopotamus
ape	jackal	python	impala	dromedary	monkey
serval	gnu	elephant	cheetah	chimpanzee	

A. p e
B. a b o o n
C. h e e t a h
D. r o m e d a r y
E. l e p h a n t
F. l a m i n g o
G. i r a f f e
H. i p p o p o t a m u s
I. m p a l a
J. a c k a l
L. e o p a r d
M. o n k e y

MYSTERY WORD: E y a d n g e r d e

Thinking Further: Imagine that you are a Kenyan in charge of finding ways to educate the public about preserving the animal population. On a separate sheet, write a paragraph that you think will help people understand the importance of saving the animals.

AFRICAN ECONOMIES

CHAPTER 18

✻ The paragraph below contains information about natural resources and other products that contribute to African economies. The scrambled names of these important items are in the word box. As you read the paragraph, unscramble the names of the products or resources and write them on the lines. The first has been unscrambled for you.

lio	aloc	glod	tontoc	miadonds	burber	brimet
artulan ags	roppec	axbiute	lassi	accoa	feft	
triceelicty	neseamang	nit	ofecef	tactel	roundstung	

_____Oil_____ is an important resource in Congo, Gabon, and Nigeria. Nigeria also has vast amounts of _____. Ghana exports _____, and _____ is found in Mozambique. Important metals found in Africa south of the Sahara include _____ in Botswana, Zambia, and Zaire; _____ in Gabon; _____ in South Africa; _____ in Mozambique, and _____ in Zaire. Fine _____ is grown in Sudan and Tanzania. Tanzania is also known for its _____. _____ is an important product in Cameroon, Ethiopia, Ivory Coast, and Tanzania. _____ are found in the Central African Republic and South Africa. _____ is a leading export of Cameroon, Ivory Coast, and Ghana. Other African agricultural resources include _____ in Botswana, _____ in Cameroon, _____ in Ethiopia, and _____ in Zambia and Senegal. _____ is a valuable asset in Gabon and Congo.

Thinking Further: Identify an important natural resource of the region where you live and tell why it is important.

_____
_____
_____

Chapter 18, pages 475–494

105

NAME _____

Toward Cooperation in Africa

CHAPTER **18**

* In 1963 foreign ministers from 32 African states gathered in Addis Ababa, Ethiopia. They met to establish a new international organization called the Organization of African Unity, or OAU. The following articles are part of the OAU Charter, or constitution. Read the articles and answer the questions.

Article I. Establishment of the Organization of African Unity. The Organization to include continental African states, Madagascar, and other islands surrounding Africa.

Article II. Aims of the OAU.
1. To promote unity and solidarity among African states
2. To intensify and coordinate efforts to improve living standards in Africa
3. To defend sovereignty, territorial integrity, and independence of African states
4. To eradicate [do away with] all forms of colonialism from Africa
5. To promote international cooperation in keeping with the Charter of the United Nations

Article IV. Each independent sovereign African state shall be entitled to become a member of the Organization.

Article V. All member states shall have equal rights and duties.

---

1. What areas other than the continent of Africa are included in the OAU? _____
_____

2. Who can become a member of the OAU? _____
_____

3. What is the relationship of member states within the organization? _____
_____

4. What is the main goal of the OAU? _____
_____

5. Which other charter does the organization want to follow? _____

Thinking Further: Describe an international organization other than the OAU or the United Nations.

_____
_____
_____

Major Cities of Asia

CHAPTER 19

✱ The list below shows the largest cities in ten Asian countries. Complete the bar graph of the populations of these cities.

a. Write the names of the cities in the blanks next to the chart. Put the cities in the order of their populations, with the most populous city at the top.

b. Shade in a bar to the right of each city's name to show its population. The first one has been done for you.

Bangkok, Thailand: 5,620,000
Beijing, China: 5,770,000
Bombay, India: 9,926,000
Delhi, India: 7,175,000
Karachi, Pakistan: 7,000,000

Jakarta, Indonesia: 8,259,000
Seoul, South Korea: 10,613,000
Shanghai, China: 7,497,000
Tokyo, Japan: 8,129,000
Tianjin, China: 4,575,000

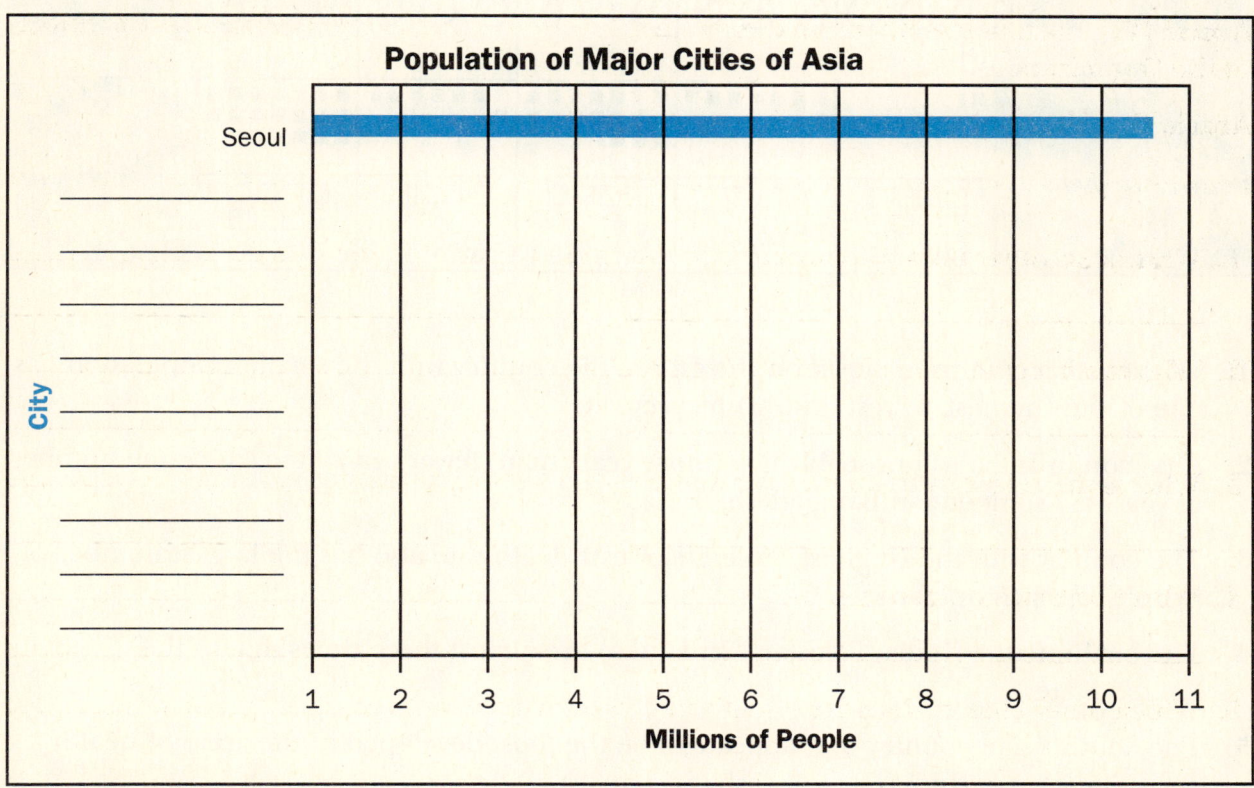

Thinking Further: How might cities like Seoul and Bombay be different from cities like Bangkok and Beijing?

Analyzing Statistics

CHAPTER 19

✳ The pictograph below compares health and education statistics for the countries of the South Asian subcontinent and the United States in the mid 1990s. Study the graph; then complete the sentences that follow by circling the correct answer in parentheses.

COUNTRY	UNITED STATES	INDIA	BANGLADESH	PAKISTAN	SRI LANKA	KEY
POPULATION (in millions)	261	920	125	122	18	
Birth rate per 1,000	○◖	○○○	○○○◖	○○○○◖	○○	○ 10
Death rate per 1,000	●●	●●	●●◖	●●●◖	●◖	● 5
Life expectancy at birth	🕐🕐🕐🕐	🕐🕐🕐	🕐🕐🕐	🕐🕐🕐	🕐🕐🕐🕐	🕐 20 years
Number of people per doctor	■▪	■■■■■■■▪	■■■■■■■■■■■▪	■■■■■■■▪	■■■■■■■■■■■	■ 300
Literacy rate	☐☐☐☐☐☐☐☐☐	☐☐☐☐☐	☐☐☐☐☐	☐☐☐☐	☐☐☐☐☐☐☐☐	☐ 10 percent

1. Of the Asian countries shown on the graph, the country with the smallest population has one of the (highest/lowest/fastest) literacy rates.

2. A person in India will probably live (more years than/fewer years than/the same number of years as) someone in Bangladesh.

3. The country with the (highest/lowest/slowest) death rate also has the largest number of people for each doctor.

4. The birthrates in (India/Pakistan/Sri Lanka) are almost three times that of the United States.

5. The South Asian country that appears to be the most developed in the areas of health and education is (India/Bangladesh/Sri Lanka).

Thinking Further: What might statistics on the number of people per doctor tell you about the quality of health care in a country?

_____

_____

_____

NAME _____

CHAPTER 19

ISLAND NATIONS OF ASIA

* Study the chart about five Asian island nations. Then read the following sentences and circle the nation or nations described.

Country	Area	Neighbor Countries	Topography
Indonesia	741,101 sq. mi.	Malaysia to the northwest, Papua New Guinea to the east	13,667 islands; 3,000 are inhabited
Maldives	115 sq. mi.	India to the northeast	2,000 islands; 220 are inhabited
Papua New Guinea	178,703 sq. mi.	Indonesia to the west, Australia to the south	Eastern half of New Guinea plus other islands
Philippines	115,800 sq. mi.	Malaysia and Indonesia to south, Taiwan to the north	7,109 islands; most people live on the 11 largest
Singapore	240 sq. mi.	Indonesia to the southeast, Malaysia to the north	Small island at the end of Malay Peninsula

1. This country contains the fewest square miles:
   Singapore   Maldives   Papua New Guinea   Philippines   Indonesia

2. This country contains the most square miles:
   Singapore   Maldives   Papua New Guinea   Philippines   Indonesia

3. This country has an area nearest 200,000 square miles:
   Singapore   Maldives   Papua New Guinea   Philippines   Indonesia

4. These countries have an area of 100,000 to 200,000 square miles:
   Singapore   Maldives   Papua New Guinea   Philippines   Indonesia

5. These countries have Indonesia as a neighbor:
   Singapore   Maldives   Papua New Guinea   Philippines   Indonesia

6. This country is a neighbor of Australia:
   Singapore   Maldives   Papua New Guinea   Philippines   Indonesia

7. This country is a neighbor of India:
   Singapore   Maldives   Papua New Guinea   Philippines   Indonesia

8. This country is made up of the most islands:
   Singapore   Maldives   Papua New Guinea   Philippines   Indonesia

Thinking Further: Imagine that you meet a person who wants to learn about Indonesia. What three or four facts about Indonesia would you mention? Write your answer on a separate sheet.

NAME _____

CHAPTER 19

TEMPERATURES IN ASIA

✱ Use the information in the bar graph to help you answer the questions below about January temperatures in Asia.

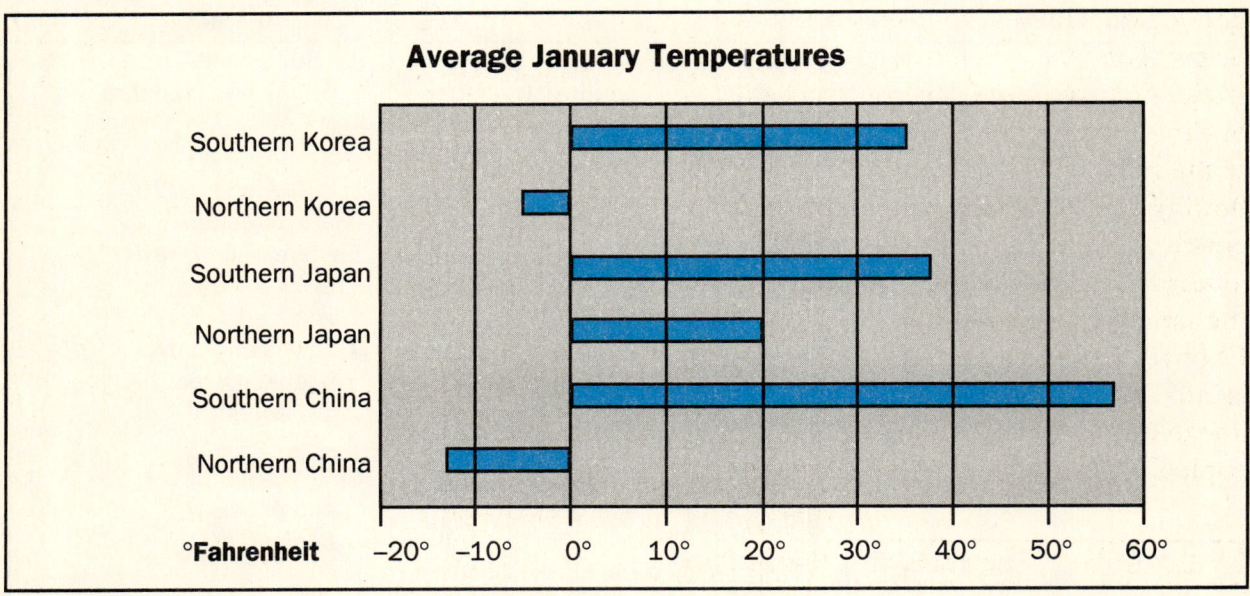

1. Which of the areas listed on the chart has the highest average temperature in January?
   _____

2. On average, how much colder is northern China than southern China in January? _____

3. If a group of people traveled from southern Japan to southern Korea in January, how could they expect the temperature to change? _____

4. If you were planning a trip to both northern and southern areas, in which country would you find the combined average temperature the highest? _____

5. In which country on the graph is the temperature change from north to south greatest?
   _____

6. If you traveled the length of all the countries from north to south in January, what would you discover about the change of temperature? _____
   _____

7. In which country is the difference between temperatures between north and south the smallest? _____

Thinking Further: Describe two or three aspects of geography that can affect an area's temperature. Write your answer on a separate sheet.

NAME _____

CHAPTER 20

WRITING WITH STYLE

✻ The Chinese people have kept written records for thousands of years. During this time, different writing styles have developed. Three of these styles are shown below. The seal style was used to copy ancient images found on bone, stone, or bronze. Most people used the broad strokes of the regular style for normal writing. The flowing grass style can express the writer's personality and mood in poetry and in letters to friends. All three columns read the same: "house full of precious things." Choose one of the three styles below. Copy it into the blank column to the right. Label it with the name of the style you have copied.

Seal Style	Regular Style	Grass Style
金	金	金
玉	玉	玉
滿	滿	滿
堂	堂	堂

Thinking Further: Where do you think the phrase you have copied might have been found?

_____
_____
_____
_____

Chapter 20, pages 527–531

THE TRAVELS OF MARCO POLO

CHAPTER 20

✱ The map below shows the areas traveled by Marco Polo. Using the description, mark the course of his journey on the map. Show the direction he traveled with arrows.

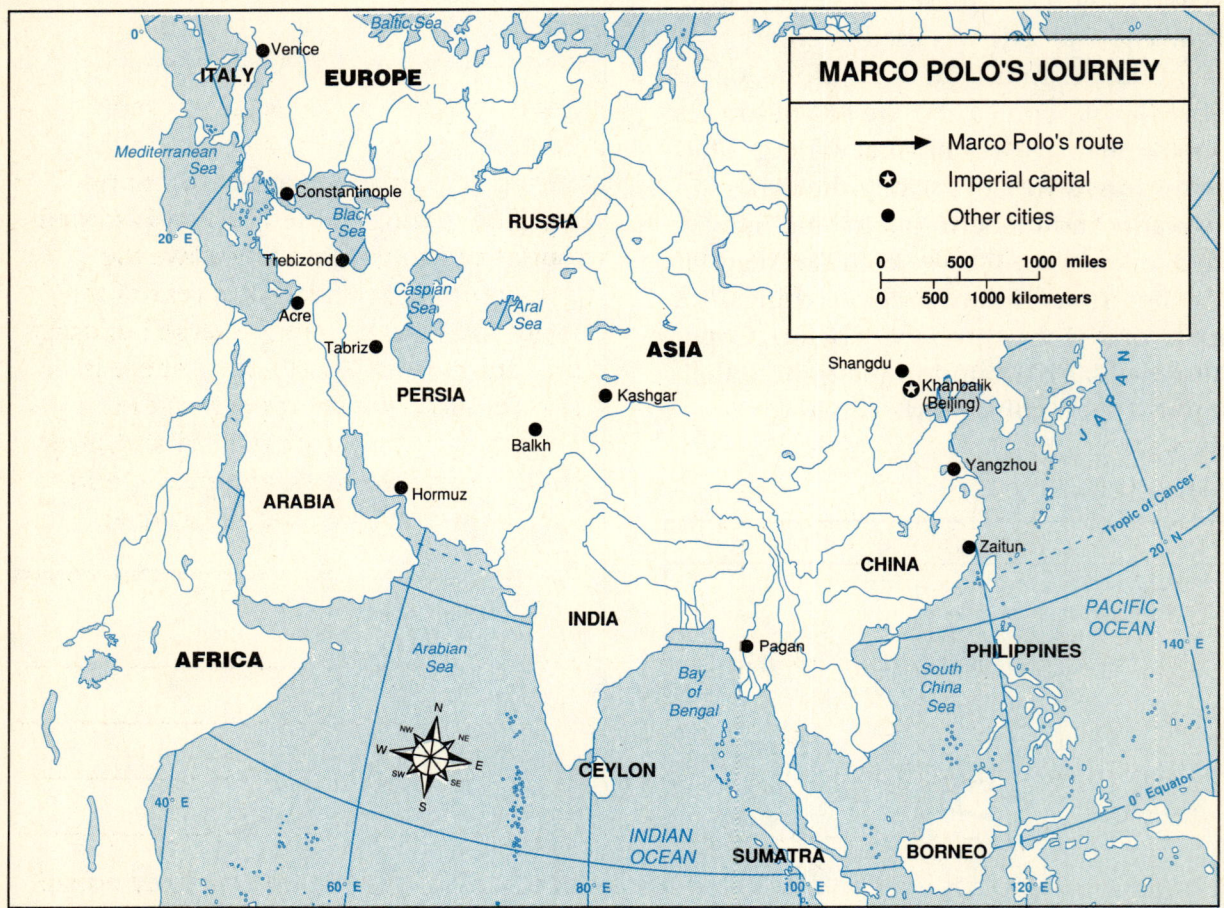

In 1271, 17-year-old Marco Polo left his home in Venice and sailed to Acre. From there, he rode in a camel caravan through Tabriz to the port city of Hormuz. He then traveled across Asia, passing through Balkh and Kashgar on his way to Shangdu. After three years of traveling he reached Shangdu, where he was welcomed into the summer palace of Kublai Khan by the emperor himself. During his stay in China, Marco Polo went to Beijing, visited Pagan, then returned to Beijing. He went to Yangzhou, where he served as a government official for three years.

After 21 years in China, Marco Polo began the trip back to Venice, traveling by sea. He departed from the port city of Zaitun and sailed through the South China Sea, around the peninsula north of Sumatra, and into the Bay of Bengal. The ships sailed between Ceylon and India, then across the Arabian Sea to Hormuz. From there, Marco Polo rode in a camel caravan through Tabriz to Trebizond, a port on the Black Sea. Boarding a ship once again, he sailed to Constantinople, then home to Venice.

NAME _____

> ## The Travels of Marco Polo continued

✴ During Marco Polo's travels in China, he visited the palace of Kublai Khan. The passage below is from *The Travels of Marco Polo*. It describes what Marco Polo saw at the palace. Read the passage, and then answer the questions.

The sides of the great halls and the apartments are ornamented with dragons in carved work and gilt, figures of warriors, of birds, and of beasts, with representations of battles.... The grand hall is extremely long and wide, and admits of dinners being there served to great multitudes of people. The palace contains a number of separate chambers, all highly beautiful, and so admirably disposed that it seems impossible to suggest any improvement to the system of their arrangement. The exterior of the roof is adorned with a variety of color, red, green, azure, and violet, and the sort of covering is so strong as to last for many years. The glazing of the windows is so well wrought and so delicate as to have the transparency of crystal. In the rear of the body of the palace there are large buildings containing several apartments, where is deposited the private property of the monarch, or his treasure in gold and silver bullion, precious stones, and pearls, and also his vessels of gold and silver plate.

---

1. What is Marco Polo's overall opinion of the palace? _____
_____

2. Where might a feast take place in the palace? _____
_____

3. What words does Marco Polo use to say that a certain part of the palace is without equal?
_____

4. What things are represented in the decorations on the palace walls? _____
_____

5. Where is the private treasure of Kublai Khan kept? _____
_____

Thinking Further: Why did many people think Marco Polo's stories were so fantastic?
_____
_____
_____

Facts About South Asia

CHAPTER 20

✱ This worksheet reviews some important facts about South Asia. After completing the sentences, decode two messages. Fill in the missing word or words to complete the statements below. Place one letter in each blank.

1. The first Portuguese explorer to arrive in South Asia was __ __ __ __(10) __ __ __ __ __(12) __.
2. The Mogul leader who invaded the Asian subcontinent was __ __ __(4) __ __.
3. The noisy Mogul weapon that frightened the elephants was the __ __ __ __ __(16) __.
4. Akbar tried to unite two religious groups: the __(3) __ __ __(17) __ __ and the __(23) __ __ __ __ __.
5. The temple built by Shah Jahan as a memorial to his wife was the __(5) __ __ __(1) __ __(25).
6. Europeans went to Asia looking for pepper, ginger, and other __(2) __(13) __ __ __.
7. The Moguls gave great encouragement to writers, craftspersons, and __ __ __ __ __ __(8).
8. India gradually came under the control of __(21) __ __ __ __ __ __ __ __ __(24).
9. The Spanish conquered the Philippines, which they named after their __(26) __ __ __(14).
10. Vietnam, Laos, and Cambodia were conquered by __ __ __ __ __(6).

✱ Use the numbered letters above to decode the messages below.

__(1) __(26) __(4) __(1) __(21) was __(5) __(3) __(6) __(14) __(21) __(6) __(1) __(5) __(6) __(8) __(5) of the __(12) __(16) __(14) __(23) __(25) __(21) __(23) __(25) __(6) __(21) __(8).

Many __(6) __(23) __(21) __(16) __(2) __(6) __(1) __(24) __(10) __(16) __(23) __(24) __(5) __(21) __(13) __(6) __(8) __(6) __(8) __(5) __(1) __(4) __(25) __(13) __(8) __(3) __(6) __(17) __(8) __(6) __(5) __(5) __(25) __(6) __(12) __(6) __(24) __(5) __(8) in __(8) __(16) __(23) __(5) __(3) __(1) __(8) __(13) __(1).

Thinking Further: Akbar tried to unite people of different faiths by inventing a new religion. Why do you think this idea failed?

_____

_____

A Changing China

CHAPTER 21

* The People's Republic of China was formed in 1949. In the years since then, some of China's Communist leaders have tried to follow socialism strictly, while others have worked to modernize China by allowing more individual freedom and trade with other nations. Ten important events in Communist China's history are listed below. Place the letter of each event in the correct box on the time line. Then answer the questions that follow.

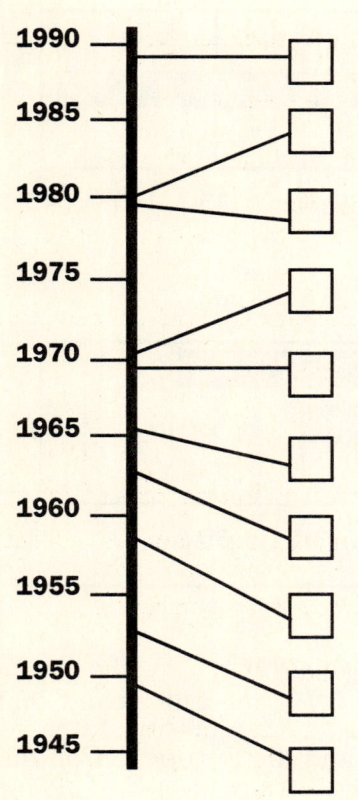

A. Communists launch the Great Leap Forward, a plan to make China a developed nation quickly—1958

B. Premier Zhou Enlai begins to expand China's diplomatic and trade contacts with other nations—1969

C. The United States and China establish normal diplomatic relations—1979

D. Mao Ze-dong proclaims establishment of the People's Republic of China—1949

E. Friendly relations between the Soviet Union and China end—1963

F. Deng Xiaoping becomes China's most powerful leader and begins program of modernization—1980

G. Student demonstration in Tiananmen Square crushed—1989

H. People's Republic of China admitted to the United Nations in place of Taiwan—1971

I. Under Communist rule, China begins its first Five-Year Plan for industrial development—1953

J. Cultural Revolution brings a return to strict socialism—1966

1. Which two events brought less freedom to the Chinese people? _____

2. How long did it take for the United States to establish diplomatic relations with the People's Republic of China? _____

3. Which economic program was designed to get immediate results? _____

Thinking Further: Why could it be difficult to lead a nation like China?

_____

_____

UNDERSTANDING JAPAN'S TRADE SUCCESS

CHAPTER 21

✱ Since World War II, Japan has become a world economic leader. One of the reasons for its success has been the strength of its foreign trade. The graphs below show Japan's main trading partners. Study the graphs and underline the correct answer to each question.

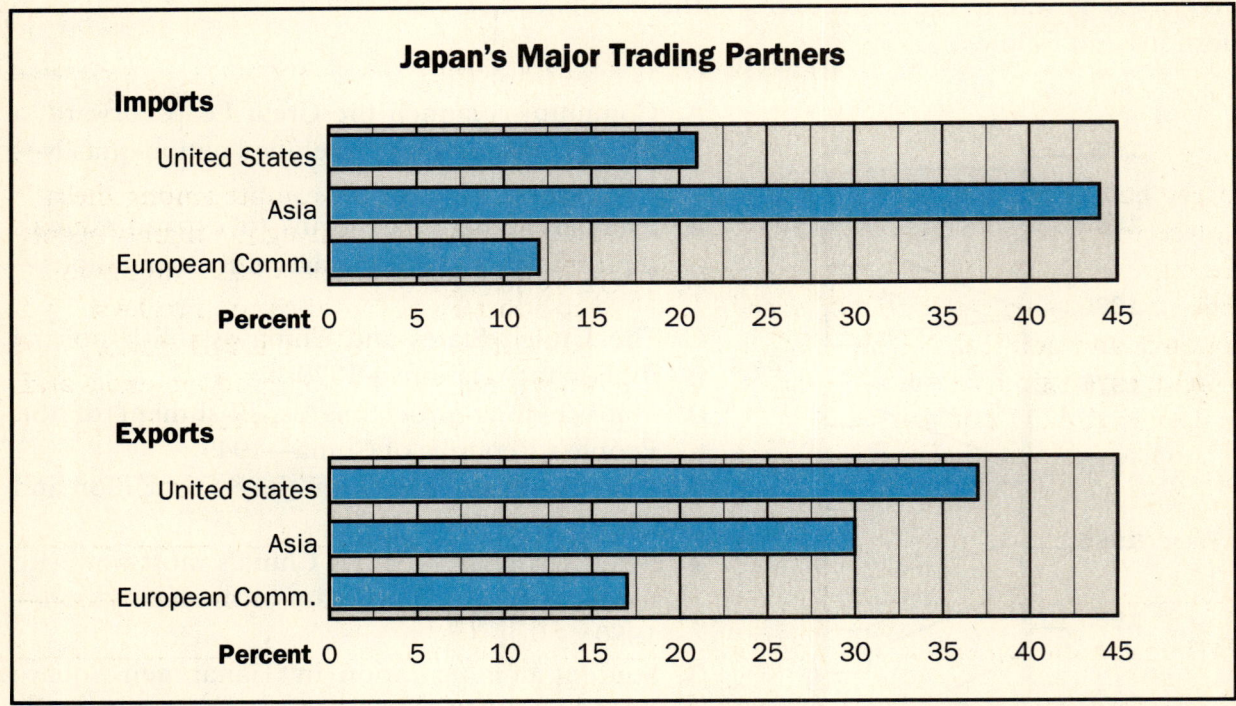

1. From where does the largest percentage of Japan's imports come?
   United States   Asia   European Community

2. What percent of Japan's exports go to the United States and the European Community?
   12%   37%   54%   72%

3. What percent of Japan's imports come from Asia?
   12%   30%   37%   44%

4. With which partner does Japan have the most even balance of imports and exports?
   United States   Asia   European Community

5. Which partner has the greatest total trade with Japan?
   United States   Asia   European Community

Thinking Further: Japan exports many more goods than it imports. Is this good or bad for Japan? Explain your reasons.

NAME _____

CHAPTER 21

WE, THE PEOPLE

✽ The constitution of a country is a written plan for the country's government. It describes how leaders will be chosen, how laws will be made, and who will make sure the laws are obeyed. Most constitutions also have a preamble, or opening statement that explains the purpose of the government. Read the preamble to India's constitution. Then answer the questions.

Preamble to the Constitution of the Republic of India

We, the people of India, have solemnly resolved to constitute [form] India into a sovereign [free] democratic republic and to secure to all its citizens: JUSTICE, social, economic and political; LIBERTY of thought, expression, belief, faith and worship; EQUALITY of status and of opportunity; and to promote among them all FRATERNITY assuring the dignity of the individual and the unity of the Nation; in our Constituent [authorized to make a constitution] Assembly this 26th day of November 1949 do hereby adopt, enact and give to ourselves this Constitution.

1. Who made the decision to set up a new government for India? _____

2. When did India adopt its constitution? _____

3. What four main things do the people of India want for all India's citizens? _____

4. What type of government does the constitution of India set up? _____

5. What do you think equality of opportunity means? _____

6. What will happen if the people of India have fraternity, or common interests and goals? _____

7. Who adopted this constitution for the people of India? _____

Thinking Further: Why is it important to know the purposes of an organization? _____

COMMUNICATING IN ASIA

CHAPTER 21

✳ In some countries people have ready access to telephones, radios, televisions, and other means of communication, while in other countries these items are not widely available. The chart below shows how many people there are for each radio, television, and telephone in six Asian countries. Study the chart and answer the questions.

Country	Number of people for each...		
	Radio	Television	Telephone
China	4.2	12.0	149.0
South Korea	1.1	4.9	4.5
Japan	1.3	3.9	1.8
Pakistan	20.0	57.0	168.0
Taiwan	1.4	3.2	3.2
India	15.0	84.0	192.0

1. How many radios would an average group of 100 Pakistani people have? _____

2. About how many radios would an average group of 100 South Koreans have? _____

3. Which nation listed has the fewest televisions per person? _____

4. Do people in Japan have more televisions or more telephones? _____

5. The six countries listed can be divided easily into two groups. List the countries in each group and describe the difference between them. _____

_____

_____

6. Why do you think there is such a difference between these two groups? _____

_____

_____

Thinking Further: How do you think the United States compares to the nations above in the number of radios, televisions, and telephones?

_____

_____

_____

POLITICAL CHANGES IN ASIA

CHAPTER 21

✱ After World War II, many nations in Asia gained their independence from Western nations. Using the map, draw a line from each Asian nation listed below to the nation from which it became independent.

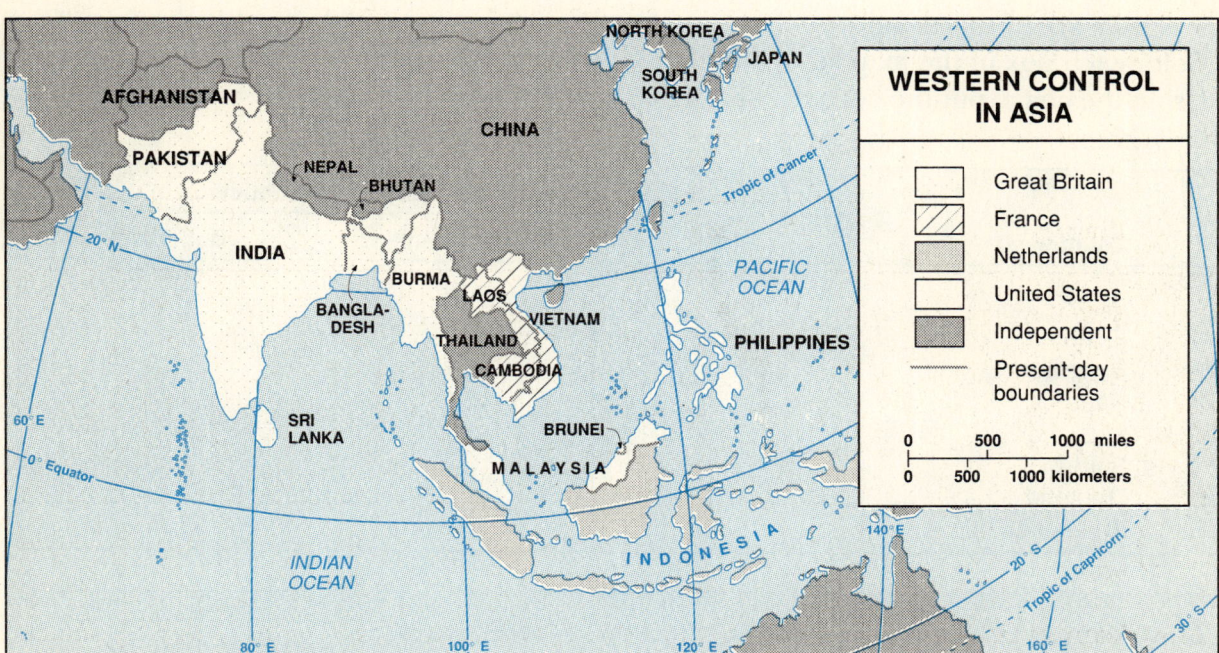

Date of Independence	Nation	Became Independent From
August 15, 1947	India	
August 14, 1947	Pakistan	
March 1971	Bangladesh	Great Britain
January 1948	Burma (Myanmar)	
July 1954	Vietnam	Netherlands
July 1949	Laos	
November 1953	Cambodia	France
July 1946	Philippines	
February 1948	Sri Lanka	United States
December 1949	Indonesia	

✱ List the nations above in the order they became independent.

_____

Thinking Further: Why did some areas controlled by Western nations divide into smaller countries after they became independent?

_____

NAME _____

CHAPTER 21

THE RELIGIONS OF SOUTH ASIA

✳ Religion has been a vital part of life in South Asia for centuries. In many countries, most people follow one religion. Study the chart and complete the map. (An asterisk [*] on the chart means that none or only a few people are of that religion.)

a. Color each box in the map key a different color.
b. Using the chart, put the correct color in each country on the map.

Country	Number of people (in millions) who follow ...		
	Islam	Hinduism	Buddhism
India	88.4	643.4	5.5
Pakistan	105.9	*	*
Bangladesh	93.4	13.1	*
Nepal	0.5	16.1	1.0
Myanmar	1.5	*	35.7
Bhutan	*	0.3	1.0
Thailand	2.1	*	52.1
Sri Lanka	1.2	2.6	11.5

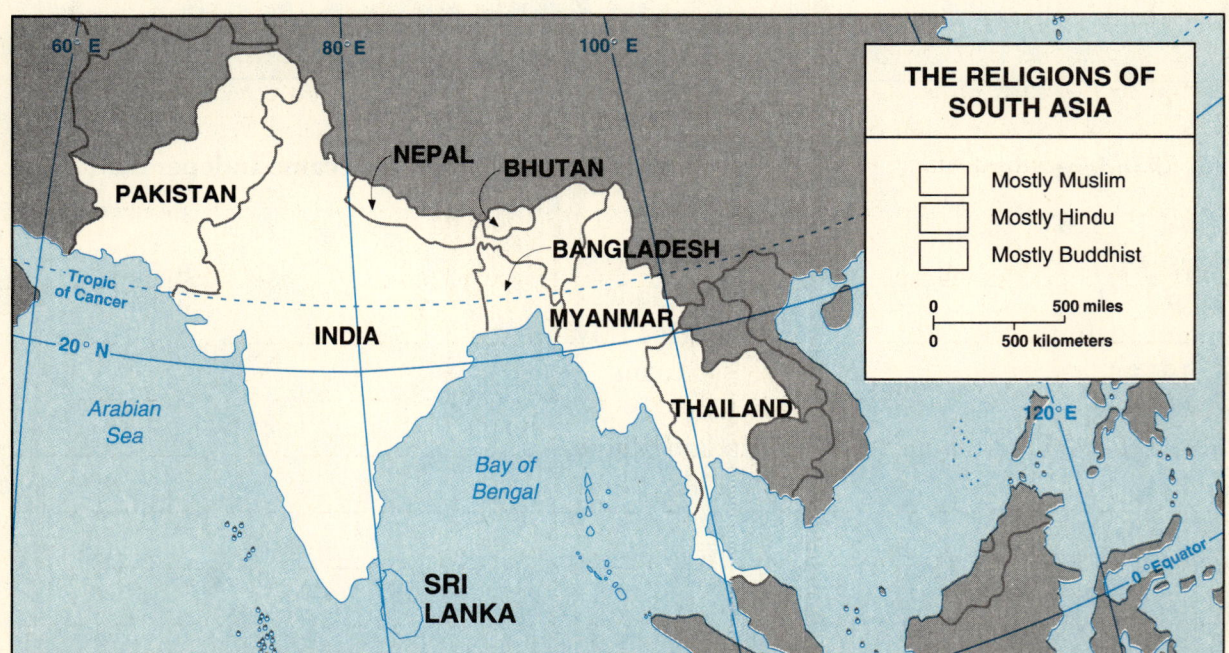

Thinking Further: How do you think religion has influenced political boundaries in South Asia?

_____

_____

NAME _____

THE GREAT BARRIER REEF

CHAPTER **22**

❋ Read the following paragraphs about Australia's Great Barrier Reef. Then answer the questions based on the passage.

The Great Barrier Reef lies off the northeast coast of Australia. It is a series of coral islands, reefs, and shoals that extend for about 1,250 miles (2,000 km). The reef is made up of billions of live corals and shells of dead corals. Scientists believe that the Great Barrier Reef began forming millions of years ago during the Ice Age.

The Aborigines were the reef's earliest human inhabitants. Many of them moved to the Australian continent when a rising ocean covered their homes on the reef. Pictures painted on the walls of caves and rocks, many of them now under water, were drawn by Aborigines thousands of years ago.

The reef was first explored and charted by Captain James Cook in 1770. His ship, the *Endeavor,* ran aground on the reef. Cook navigated his way out of the reef by discovering a channel of deeper water. This channel was named Cook's Passage. It is still used today.

The Great Barrier Reef is a big tourist attraction. At high tide, it is 90 percent under water. At low tide, people can walk on the reef and observe the plant and animal life. Some people scuba dive or fish. More species of plant and animal life live on the reef than almost anywhere else in the world.

Unfortunately, the reef is now threatened. Sewage and pesticides from coastal cities and farms are released into the reef area. Companies have come to explore for oil. To help prevent further damage to the reef, the Australian government passed the Great Barrier Marine Park Act, in 1975, to protect life on the reef.

1. What are the islands and reefs of the Great Barrier Reef made of? _____

2. When did the reef begin forming? _____

3. How do we know about the reef's first inhabitants? _____

4. Why is Captain Cook important to the history of the reef? _____

5. What do people enjoy doing on the reef? _____

6. How is the reef being threatened today? _____

Thinking Further: Why is it important to preserve a natural feature like the Great Barrier Reef and protect its wildlife? Use a separate sheet.

NAME _____

CHAPTER 22

CHANGES IN NEW ZEALAND'S TRADE

✱ The pie graphs below show New Zealand's main trading partners in 1984 and 1988. Use the information for 1988 to complete the 1988 graph; then answer the questions that follow.

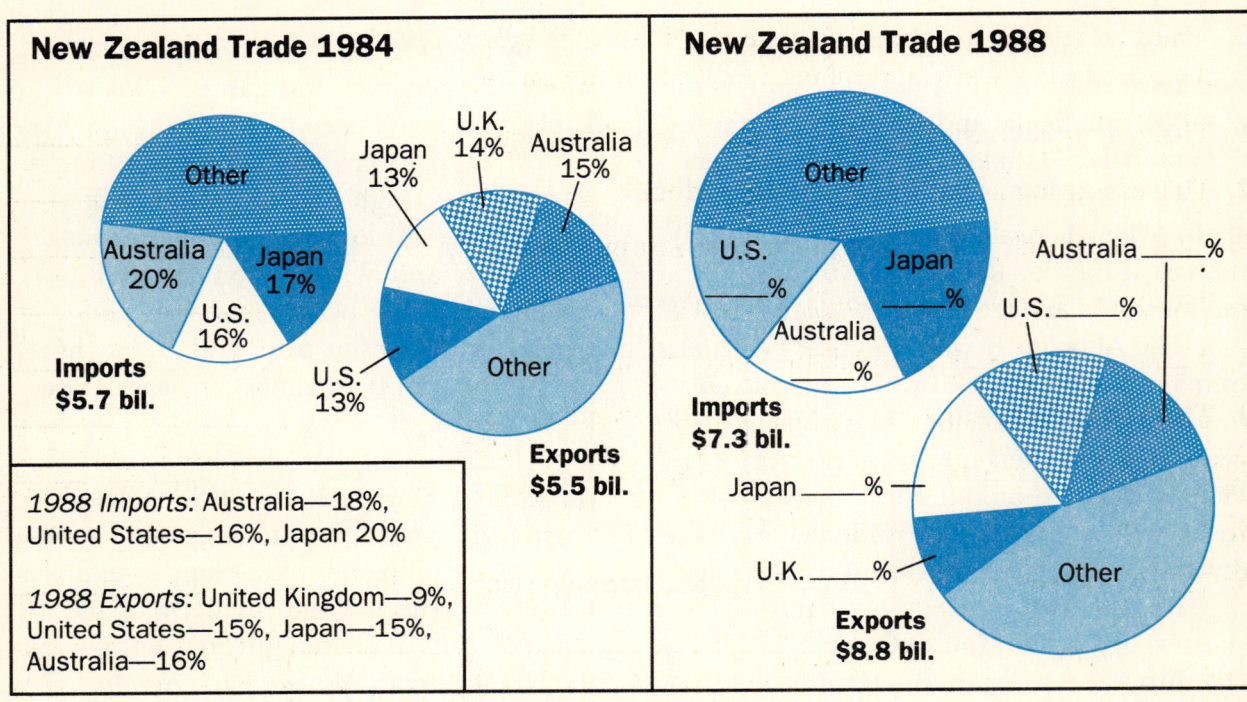

1988 Imports: Australia—18%, United States—16%, Japan 20%

1988 Exports: United Kingdom—9%, United States—15%, Japan—15%, Australia—16%

1. How did the total value of imports and exports change from 1984 to 1988? _____

2. Did imports or exports show a greater increase? _____

3. How did New Zealand's import partners change during the period shown? _____

4. How did export partners change? _____

5. How did New Zealand's imports from the United States change during the four-year period?

6. How did New Zealand's exports to the United States change? _____

Thinking Further: Based on the information above, do you think New Zealand's trade with the United States changed greatly between 1988 and 1992? Explain your answer. Use a separate sheet.

NAME _____

WILDLIFE OF AUSTRALIA AND NEW ZEALAND

CHAPTER 22

✻   The statements below describe some of the many interesting birds and animals that live in Australia and New Zealand.
a. Write the name of the correct bird or animal in the blank next to each description.
b. Place each name on the correct line in the puzzle below. Use the length of the names and the letters given on the puzzle as clues.

1. This marsupial has short front legs and large back legs. _____
2. This egg-laying animal has a bill like a duck. _____
3. Like the ostrich, this large bird can run fast but cannot fly. _____
4. This furry, tree-dwelling animal looks like—but is not—a bear. _____
5. This noisy bird is nicknamed the "laughing jackass." _____
6. This egg-laying animal is also known as the "spiny anteater." _____
7. This large New Zealand bird is now extinct. _____
8. This animal is also known as the "flying possum." _____
9. This small flightless bird is New Zealand's national symbol. _____

Thinking Further: Why do you think Australia and New Zealand have so many birds and animals that appear nowhere else on the earth?

_____
_____
_____

Chapter 22, pages 573–581   123

NAME _____

CHAPTER 22

GEOGRAPHY OF THE PACIFIC ISLANDS

* Complete the sentences below to decode a message about the origin of the South Pacific Islands.

a. Complete each sentence by choosing the correct word from the word box. Write one letter of the word in each blank.

b. Use the numbered letters to decode the message. Some letters have been given.

TROPICAL   MELANESIA   ATOLLS

TYPHOON   NEW GUINEA

POLYNESIA   DATELINE   MICRONESIA

---

1. _ _ _ _ _ _ _ _ _ _ means "small islands."
   14

2. The climate of the Pacific Islands is _ _ _ _ _ _ _ _.
   23

3. Ringlike islands formed by coral are called _ _ _ _ _ _.
   8

4. In the Pacific a hurricane is called a _ _ _ _ _ _ _.
   10

5. _ _ _ _ _ _ _ _ _ means "many islands."
   65

6. The 180° meridian is called the International _ _ _ _ _ _ _ _.
   1411

7. _ _ _ _ _ _ _ is the largest of the Pacific Islands.
   1312

8. _ _ _ _ _ _ _ _ _ means "black islands."
   97

$\underline{}\ \underline{}\ \underline{}\ \underline{}\quad \underline{}\ \underline{}\ \underline{}\ \underline{}\ \underline{}\ \underline{}\quad \underline{}\ \underline{}\ \underline{}\ \underline{}$
 1 2 8 11   7 8 6 9 12 14 8   13 5 4 5

$\underline{F}\ \underline{}\ \underline{}\ \underline{}\ \underline{}\quad \underline{B}\ \underline{}\quad \underline{V}\ \underline{}\ \underline{}\ \underline{}\ \underline{}\ \underline{}\ \underline{}$
    2 4 1 5 14   10   2 6 3 9 12 2 5 8

$\underline{}\ \underline{}\quad \underline{}\ \underline{}\ \underline{}\ \underline{}\quad \underline{}\ \underline{}\ \underline{F}\ \underline{}$
 2 4   3 2 4 9 6   4 5 5   8

Thinking Further: Why do you think the Pacific Islands have been called the "lands of endless summer?"

_____

_____

_____

NAME _____

CHAPTER 23

FINDING DISTANCES IN EASTERN AUSTRALIA

* The map below shows eastern Australia. Use the map scale to determine the distance between the places mentioned in the statements. Underline or fill in the best answers.

1. The distance from Brisbane to the Tropic of Capricorn is about

   <u>450 miles</u>   275 miles

2. The distance between Canberra and Mount Kosciusko is just under

   200 miles   <u>100 miles</u>

3. The distance from Melbourne to the northern tip of Tasmania is about

   <u>350 km</u>   500 km

4. The distance from the tip of the Cape York Peninsula to the Mitchell River is about

   250 miles   <u>350 miles</u>

5. The distance from the capital city of Victoria to the capital city of New South Wales is about

   <u>600 miles</u>   450 miles

6. The distance from Newcastle to Canberra is about

   <u>375 km</u>   275 km

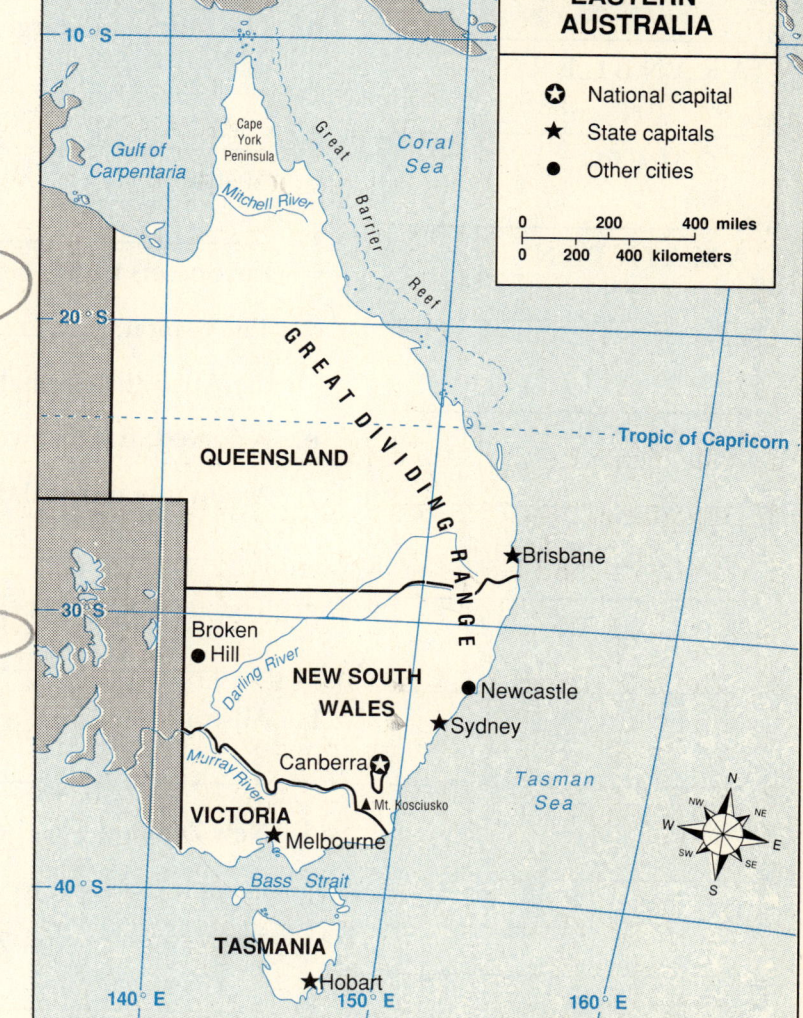

7. The distance from Hobart in Tasmania to Melbourne is about _____ miles.

8. The distance from Broken Hill to the Murray River is about _____ km.

Thinking Further: What things would you like to see if you visited Australia?

AUSTRALIA AND NEW ZEALAND

CHAPTER 23

✱ Can you figure out the words that help describe Australia and New Zealand? If so, you can complete the statements below.
a. Unscramble the words under each blank in the left column.
b. Complete the sentences in the right column by putting the unscrambled letters in the correct blank.

1. _____
   A R A N B C E R
2. _____
   R O M A I S
3. _____
   A M A I A T S N
4. _____
   N D S Y E Y
5. _____
   K O C O
6. _____
   E F E B
7. _____
   W N G E L T L I O N
8. _____
   N T I N C O N E T
9. _____
   G O A B R I I N E S
10. _____
    L O G D
11. _____
    N R E O M B A O G
12. _____
    E O T V

a. The oldest and largest Australian city is _____.

b. _____ is an island that is part of Australia.

c. _____ lived in Australia before Europeans came.

d. The capital, _____, is located in the Australia Capital Territory.

e. A curved, flat throwing stick is a _____.

f. A valuable mineral discovered in Australia in 1851 was _____.

g. The early settlers of New Zealand were _____.

h. Australia leads the world in the production of _____.

i. New Zealand was the first country in the world to give women the right to _____.

j. The capital of New Zealand is _____.

k. _____ explored the coasts of Australia and New Zealand.

l. Australia is both a country and a _____.

Thinking Further: Do you think the vast interior of Australia will remain unsettled? Give reasons for your answer.

_____
_____
_____

Lands of the Pacific

CHAPTER 23

* Use the clues below to complete the crossword puzzle about Australia, New Zealand, and the Pacific Islands.

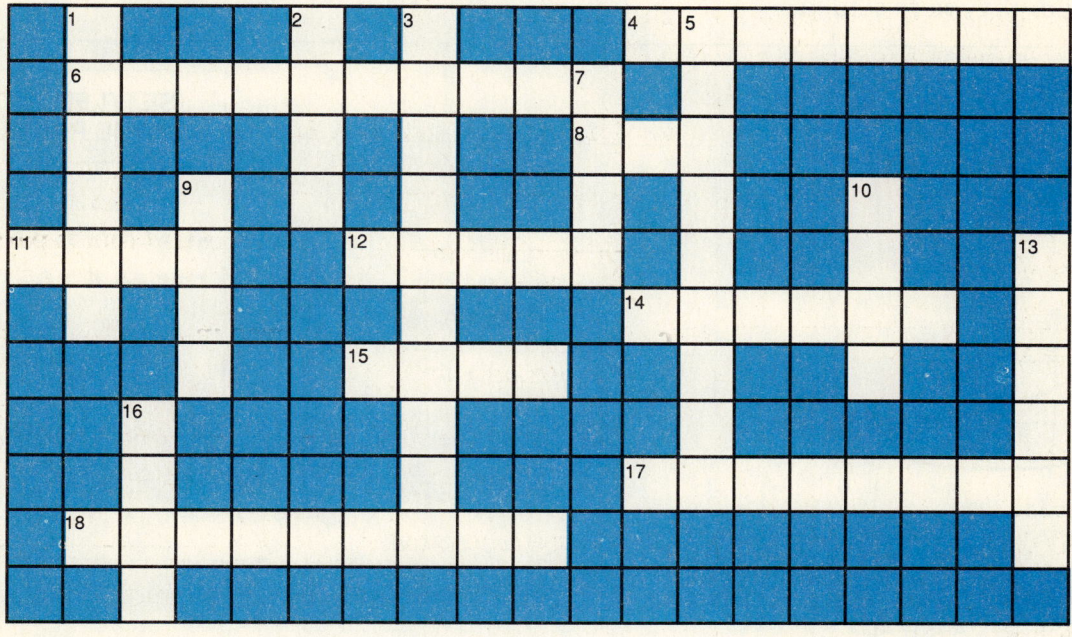

ACROSS

4. Disease brought by Europeans
6. Native people of Australia
8. Important resource of Papua New Guinea
11. Fruit grown in New Zealand, named after a bird
12. Gilbert Islands are reefs made of this
14. Meat from sheep
15. Australia leads the world in the export of this
17. Culture handed down from the past
18. Native Australian throwing stick

DOWN

1. Became our fiftieth state in 1959
2. Used to clear the forests of New Zealand
3. Vast Pacific region of small islands
5. Large city on south coast of Australia
7. Wind blows this away when ground is dry
9. British colony in Melanesia that became independent in 1974
10. First English explorer of Australia
13. Most productive mine of this metal is in Australia
16. A leading export of Australia since the days of early settlers

Thinking Further: Explain how the statement "Australia is the land down under" is both correct and incorrect.

Settlement of the Pacific Islands

CHAPTER 23

* People from Asia had settled in the Pacific region long before the European explorers arrived. The map shows when people arrived on the islands of the Pacific. Use the map to number the places in each box in the order they were settled.

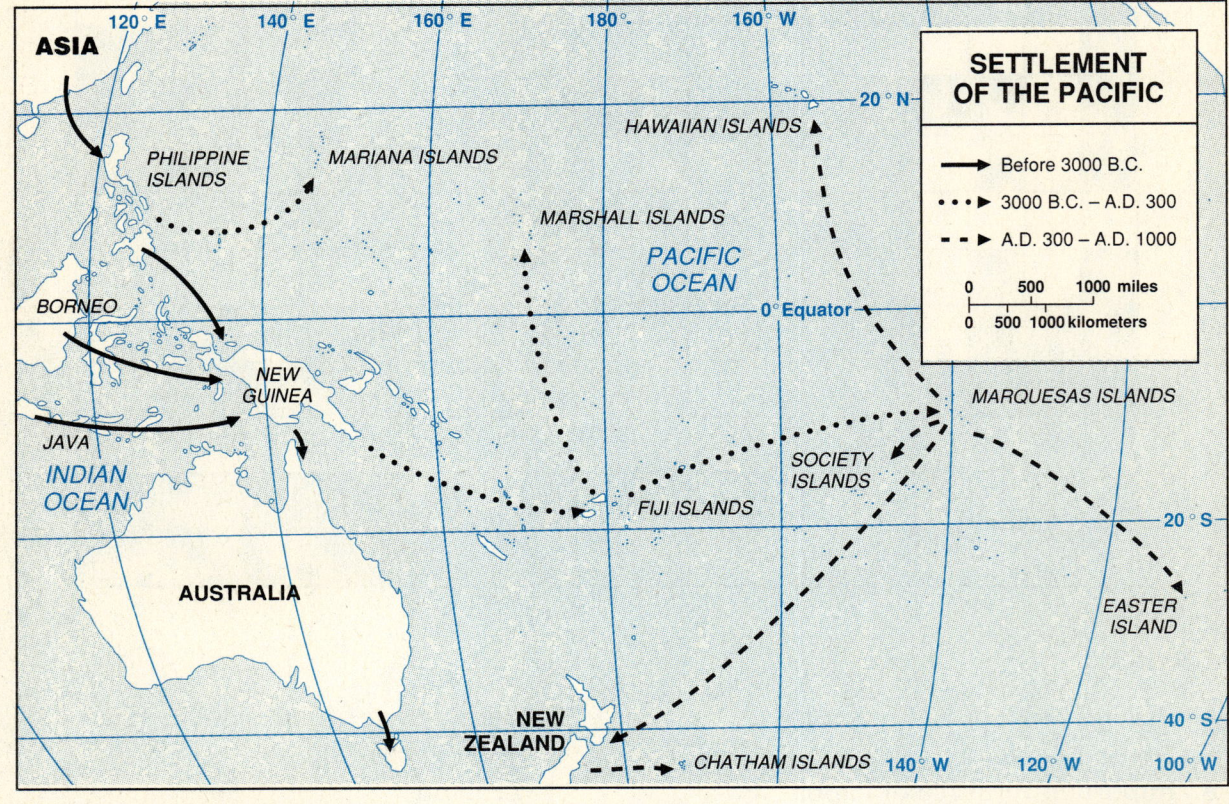

_4_ Easter Island	_4_ Society Islands	___ Chatham Islands
_1_ Borneo	_2_ New Guinea	___ Asia
_2_ Fiji Islands	_1_ Philippines	___ New Zealand
_3_ Marquesas Islands	_3_ Fiji Islands	___ New Guinea
		___ Fiji Islands
		___ Marquesas Islands

Thinking Further: Why do you think it took so long to settle the Pacific Islands?

_____
_____
_____